# PRAISE FOR THE JOURNEY TO AUTHENTICITY AND MITCHELL JONES

*The Journey to Authenticity* has many nuggets of wonderful wisdom that readers will be able to apply in every area of their lives. With Tony's guidance, Mitchell generously shares his story and accounts for mistakes made and lessons learned that leave the reader with hope for redemption and steps towards genuine...(wait for it)...AUTHENTICITY! *The Journey to Authenticity* is a great motivation to begin your own journey!

———————

This book is a good read for anyone who is seeking their true identity. While Mitchell is sharing his life and lessons, the reader can gain great knowledge from the 8 secrets to getting the life you desire! You don't have to be struggling with your sexuality to enjoy *The Journey to Authenticity*. As I have learned in life, "eat the meat and spit out the bones" to all you feel doesn't apply to you. Don't overlook the 8 lessons, they are great!

*more...*

I0113892

After reading the book, I truly feel compelled to continue what God has asked me to do, and it's such a breath of fresh air to connect with a kindred spirit. I truly feel I know [Mitchell Jones], and we've never met in person, but [his] story has touched me. [*The Journey to Authenticity*] will truly continue to help me on my journey.

# The Journey to Authenticity

*8 Secrets to Getting the Life You Desire*

MITCHELL L. JONES

*with Dr. Tony Lamair Burks II*

L3 Publishing LLC
230 West Main Street
Wakefield, Virginia 23888
209-809-1LIV

Cover Photograph by Stanz Eyez Photography
Cover Design by Laura Duffy Design

*All scriptures are from The Holy Bible, King James Version. Public Domain.*

The Journey to Authenticity: 8 Secrets to Getting the Life You Desire / Mitchell L. Jones with Dr. Tony Lamair Burks II – 1st ed. ISBN 978-0997329902

# DEDICATION

*To those who dare to LiveLifeLiv!*

**LiveLifeLiv** /liv līf līv/ ***verb. noun.***
[*Origin American. M. Jones from English,
literally, "remain alive" and "the period from birth
to death" and "not dead or inanimate"*]. 1. the
practice of living life one moment at a
time, instead of one day at a time. 2. the
willful, intentional choice to live in the
moment, not in the fear of yesterday, and
not in the anxiety of tomorrow. Ex. *By
choosing to meditate, I LiveLifeLiv.*

LIVELIFELIV

# CONTENTS

# ACKNOWLEDGEMENTS

## PASTOR MITCHELL

I crafted the broad concepts of this book in my head well before I put pen to paper or fingers to keys. Somehow Dr. Tony Lamair Burks II knew I had the *Eight Secrets* hidden within me, ready to escape. I appreciate him for introducing me to *Publishing at Sea*, hosting writing retreats, pushing my thinking, and giving me homework assignments which we transformed into *LifeWork*.

Writing this book was a sojourn of turns, twists, zags, and zigs. I have laughed out loud and wondered. I have sobbed alone and with my writing team. I have questioned my past and charted my future. The result of this experience is *The Journey to Authenticity: 8 Secrets to Getting the Life You Desire.*

I wish to thank...
- My six children for inspiring me to *LiveLifeLiv*;
- My ex-wife for her courage and understanding along the way;
- *LiveLifeLiv International Assembly for Humanity* for steadfast support in the midst of tremendous changes in consciousness;
- Shawn and Ashley Pitts-Williams for friendship and being my gateway to Atlanta;
- Thandiwe DeShazor for attention to detail and his keen sense of storytelling;
- Lori Read for her compassion and focus;

# THE JOURNEY TO AUTHENTICITY

- Stanley and Elizabeth Jones, my parents, for loving me unconditionally;
- My eight siblings—Caleb, Kenneth, Darryl, Ronnie, Stanley III, Valencia, Hope, and Michael—for great memories and experiences;
- Sandra Carrington Jordan for always being there and for embracing me just as I am;
- Michael, Sandra, and Thandiwe for reading passages of this book and offering feedback;
- *Real Husbands and Wives of Atlanta* for their loving support; and
- The faculty of *Publishing at Sea 2016* for critical friendship and solid publishing ideas.

MLJ
*Wakefield, Virginia*

---

## DOCTOR BURKS

I am thankful...
- Documentarian Timothy Daniels introduced me to Mitchell in November 2015 and invited him into our Sacred Circle.
- Actor and Writer Thandiwe DeShazor motivated me throughout this project and reminds me who I am and whose I am.
- Publishing Expert Dr. Judith Briles hosted *Publishing at Sea 2016* where Mitchell and I refined key elements of this book.

- Rev. Dr. Barbara Lewis King shared Lessons in Living at *Hillside International Truth Center*. The practical teachings of Jesus the Christ found in her sermons—along with the teachings of Sylvia High and *Aiming High*—inform my actions and writings.
- My grandparents and parents—Janice Potter Burks and Tony Lamair Burks—gave me roots *and* wings, grounding me in family and beckoning me to soar.
- Pastor Mitchell Jones entrusted me with his intriguing story. I appreciate his openness as we experimented with an array of storyWeaving tools. It's as if we've known each other for years; calling, texting, and emailing each other with flashes of insight about this book and kernels of wisdom about life.

tlb2
*Atlanta, Georgia*

# 1 FAUX-THENTICITY

**faux-thenticity** /fō THenˈtisədē/ ***noun.***
[*Origin American. M. Jones/T. Burks from
French, literally "false" and from Ancient Greek
authentikós meaning "genuine"*]. 1. the quality
or state of faking one's authenticity or
realness. 2. being artificially real; yet,
projecting an image of genuineness. 3. the
quality of being deceptively inauthentic.
Ex. . . . *I was so skilled at faux-thenticity that I
convinced myself I was authentic, even when I
knew I wasn't.*

*First things first*: My journey to authenticity began
long before I appeared on *Iyanla Fix My Life*. When
I agreed to appear on *Fix My Life*, my plan was to
take part in a general discussion about gay pastors
in the Black Church and parenting. I had been out
as a same-gender loving man since 2009, around the

time I separated from my wife. That was just over five years before any of the *Fix My Life* episodes of my story aired.

*Fix My Life* framed my sexuality as a big reveal, but it was nothing like that—such is the nature of Reality Television. This isn't an attack on the show or its team; I just seek to be clear about my truth as I see it. The *Fix My Life* team didn't lie to me or misrepresent themselves. I don't regret my choice to appear on the show, but the conversation about being gay in the Black church was minimal.

They asked me if I had cheated on my wife during our marriage. I said, "No!" Of course, this was a lie. I didn't tell the truth because I didn't think adding this point fit the narrative I was trying to present.

It's amazing what I allowed my ego to do: I convinced myself to be OK telling my story without all the facts. I believed I could do this without hurting anyone. This hidden part of me had nothing to do with the Black Church and the original reason I'd contacted the show. The more I convinced myself to be comfortable with this little white lie, the more the lie pressed against my spirit.

Days later, the truth gnawed at me. It was unrelenting. I had to come clean about the affairs I had during our five years of marriage. I had to tell the truth if I were serious about being authentic. While the producers weren't outwardly exuberant with my decision to reveal this truth, I immediately sensed they were leaping with excitement inside.

This was the juicy goodness that made for provocative television.

My ex-wife, Diamond, is a smart woman; however, we caught her off guard when I told the truth about my affairs. From our history as husband and wife, I felt the news could be quite disturbing and disconcerting. I didn't want my revelation to possibly lead either of us to depression. I figured having Iyanla Vanzant at our side was a wise choice. I knew the national broadcast would give us a safe place to share, hear, and process my lies and my truths.

My journey to authenticity began with me coming to terms with who I am as a spiritual being in the eyes of God. I had to unlearn many of the religious teachings that left me shackled and abused. Then I had to develop the courage and strength to reveal my truth. I did so at the risk of losing it all, from friends and loved ones to material things. After this phase, I came to terms with my sexuality. This allowed me to reconnect with my renewed spirit.

When I contacted Iyanla's show, I felt I pretty much had a handle on my work. I *now* know the final missing (and surprising) piece was the work I did *on* the show. I decided to appear on the show to be completely unguarded and unfettered. I didn't want to remain bound by lies blocking my growth. I desired a clear path to spiritual and emotional well-being for myself and my family.

In the months after they taped the three episodes, I pondered the value of telling my story. I needed to ask myself, *What am I here to do?* and *What is my gift?* When I finally decided to tell my story, the answer to these two questions helped me get to the core of why I felt compelled to write this book:

*What am I here to do?* I believe my purpose in life is to serve as a teaching minister. I believe I am here to grow my ministry. Part of this ministry is helping people learn that God has empowered us to be brilliant creations. I am here to help people embrace the spirit within so they may live intimately connected to God as Divine Intelligence. I am here to promote love and unity across diverse cultures, classes, religions, and races. I know we are not separated from the deep and abiding love of God. Because of this, I teach universal principles found in various faiths and traditions.

*What is my gift?* I believe God blessed me with the time-honored gift of music. The tremendous healing powers of music have existed since the beginning of life itself. The soft, gentle breeze. The swaying branches and rustling leaves on a muted autumn evening. The streams, birds, and insects performing in melodic symphony. These are God's instruments of praise. I use songs and sermons to inspire, influence, and encourage people to

live life fully. I am alive when I create through
music.

I listened to the responses of my heart, and I was
compelled to live an authentic life. I realized I
wasn't being authentic back then. I was comfortable
existing disconnected from the real me. I was
hoping no one would look beneath it all to see I
was anything but authentic. I was what I now call
*faux-thentic*: I was faking my authenticity. I was so
skilled at *faux-thenticity* that I convinced myself I was
authentic, even when I knew I wasn't.

I was living the high life. I pastored a growing
church, wore custom suits, drove the latest
"whips," and my wife and I lived in a sprawling
suburban home with our blended family of five
children. We were living a charmed existence; yet, I
was leading a double life that threatened to shatter
the very world and persona I'd worked so hard to
build. Even as I fought to *keep it on the down low*, I
longed to be real.

*The Journey to Authenticity: 8 Secrets to Getting the Life
You Desire* is a revealing look at my story and the
secrets I've used on my journey to authenticity. The
*Eight Secrets* are a way to cut through the madness
and get to the heart of it all. They stripped me
down to my essence. They saved my life. More than
anything, the *Eight Secrets* are bigger than my
sexuality. They are universal and you can apply
them to your life regardless of who you are and
where you are on your journey to authenticity. If
you focus solely on me being a same gender loving

man, you'll miss the power and promise the *Eight Secrets* could have in your life.

————

**Life·Work** /līf‚wərk/ ***noun***. *[Origin American. T. Burks from English language, literally life (n.) + work (n.); adapted from from home (n.) + work (n.), 1680s, "work done at home"]*. 1. Practical application of the *8 Secrets to Getting the Life You Desire* envisioned by Mitchell L. Jones. 2. Work or study done in preparation for *LivingLifeLiv*. 3. A reflective assignment that engages one's struggles and situational difficulties directly to foster personal growth and development. 4. Homework for living an authentic life. Ex. ...*Taken together, LifeWork and the Eight Secrets are the foundation of my never-ending journey to authenticity.*

It has taken time to understand myself and my journey. I have learned authenticity is a journey and not a destination. And if, by chance, it were a destination, that destination would be to ourselves. In this book, I share tools I am using on my journey to authenticity. The *Eight Secrets* focus on the art of *being* because often we focus on *doing* or *having* and miss out on authentic living. In essence, to live an authentic life one must *be*...

- courageous
- vulnerable
- steadfast
- forgiving
- grateful
- patient
- open
- and loving

You'll notice I didn't write one must be *more* courageous or *more* grateful. You're either courageous or you aren't; you're grateful or you're not. If I desire an authentic life, I must do my work. I call this work, *LifeWork*. This work is essential to living an authentic life. *LifeWork* involves states of being and doing, which lead to having the life one desires: *LiveLifeLiv*.

Taken together, *LifeWork* and the *Eight Secrets* are the foundation of my never-ending journey to authenticity. They are key parts of an ever-unfolding experience of noticing, analyzing, and revealing my truth.

This is my story. I hope you'll use it and the *Eight Secrets* to help you break down walls, ask yourself hard questions, and find the best *you* along the way.

# JONES

## 2 ROCK BOTTOM

"You're not clear," she told me.

"You've still got some denial and some delusion in there. Because it's just too well put together. And it's not making sense that you are not flat on your back, prostrate in your spirit, begging for forgiveness; I don't understand it."

Iyanla Vanzant was matter of fact and made it clear she was running the show.

"Have you hit Rock Bottom yet?" she later asked me.

"I'd like to think so," I sheepishly responded.

She wasn't buying it.

"When you do that level of truth telling, to the degree that you can't look at yourself in the mirror without vomiting, that's Rock Bottom. I don't think you've gotten there yet."

I nodded in agreement.

"Because you still tell the story," she blared.

"You're still holding on to the image that it's OK. I wish today was the day you would just give yourself permission to just let it all go."

She ordered me upstairs to get myself together. The cameras were off and all the crew were in another room except for one producer. She and I were conversing.

Iyanla was right. I wasn't there. And I didn't want to be there.

I thought I'd been there. I'd admitted the pain I caused myself by cheating. I'd lost my family as I knew it, my ministry, and my possessions.

I'd hit rock bottom—or so I'd thought. But I really hadn't.

I'd shared my story and my version of the truth. I hadn't confessed my cheating to my ex-wife and to my family. I wasn't being authentic and Iyanla knew it instinctively. I'd told just enough of my truth to be *near* there, but not *there*.

*There* was rock bottom.

It was a place I'd avoided.

I was not being authentic. I was only dipping a toe into the pond of full truth. Iyanla needed me to be completely invested, completely naked, completely submerged.

When I'd mapped out the journey of my life, rock bottom wasn't a part of the plan. Iyanla's hope for me to hit rock bottom to find and live my truth was a prayer, an invocation, and my soul responded.

# THE JOURNEY TO AUTHENTICITY

———————

"Never let them see you sweat," echoed in my head and heart. It's what I often saw and heard. My parents injected it into my DNA. And when I was a young child, they nurtured that value and many others.

I thought of my parents, Stanley Jones Jr. and Elizabeth Mariah Bailey Jones, when I began my journey to authenticity. Both were born in 1940 and graduated from high school in 1958. They were married in 1959, and nine children followed. My parents raised us in Wakefield, Virginia, an hour outside of Richmond. My father worked in a paper mill and my mother drove a school bus.

Even though my father retired in 2003, he's never been idle and continues to stay busy. My parents passed on their beliefs to us. They have an amazingly strong work ethic. All of us were taught to take care of ourselves and each other. Home and faith were a priority and minding our own business was a must. My parents simply wouldn't allow others to interfere with the business of our lives.

We lived a different life in a different world. My siblings and I were raised in a close-knit religious community. Our lives were lived in school and church. Between Bible study, choir rehearsals, and special services, we were in church nearly five days a week at times. I lived a sheltered life immersed in the activities of my church, which left little time for involvement elsewhere. I even sang and played piano and organ there. If I didn't see you at church or school, I didn't see you otherwise.

Church was my solace. It was the cocoon shielding my family from exposure to faith traditions unlike ours. Believe me, we had a monopoly on Jesus Christ; whatever contradicted Him and His Father's teachings was cursed. We simply didn't accept other faiths and cultures. We demonized differences, denouncing to the smoldering pit of Hell anyone or anything we didn't understand.

I was a Bible-thumping boy with a gift for singing and praising who became a preacher and taught the Gospel. It seemed like a natural thing to do. Though I felt the call to preach at a young age, I didn't preach my first sermon until I was nearly 24 years old.

I'd been flip-flopping on my decision to preach for many months and then one Sunday morning, I climbed in bed and curled up next to my brother. There's no bond like that of twins. We can sense each other's happiness and hurts. We can communicate without uttering a syllable. My mind was swirling; I felt confused and anxious. As we lay in silence, my brother gave me the final push.

"You're going to preach today, Mitchell."

Whether it was Wonder Twin Power or a psychic connection, my brother offered the confirmation I desired. And I preached that Sunday.

———

My siblings have always had a dramatic effect on my life and my decisions. I think this is the nature of many large families. The closer I got to the *Fix My Life* house, the more I wondered about my siblings. I wondered how they would respond to me after my decision to tell my truth aired on national television.

I replayed some conversations and burning questions as I walked up the stairs to the *Fix My Life* house that day:

> *What would our father think?*
> *What about our mother?*
> *What would our mother encounter at church and in the community?*
> *Why did you have to do this now, Mitchell?*

My desire to share my truth was about my healing and transformation. It was about my journey to Mitchell.

———

And then it happened without fanfare: rock bottom.

At first a tear trickled down my face; then I began to cry uncontrollably. *This* was the *there* for which Iyanla and I prayed: This was rock bottom. "Never let them see you sweat" no longer held me hostage as a childhood value. This was the emotional fall from grace that was vigilantly waiting for me to trust myself enough to let go.

True healing from a fall from grace comes when our emotional and physical elements align. True healing happens when we acknowledge moments wherein we have been inauthentic.

*Why was I crying? What caused me to double over?*

I was crying because of the things I'd experienced and what I'd lost in my life.

I'd orchestrated my fall from grace during my tenure as the fulltime pastor of a growing church. I was a married father of five healthy children. We visually represented what prayer and right living could do for you. We had whatever material possessions we desired. Our expansive home was nestled on three acres along the Chuckatuck, a picturesque creek that meanders its way out into the Nansemond River.

Ours was a *nouveau riche* lifestyle of a family that had "come into some money."

*Luxury cars? Check.*

*Multi-car garage? Check.*

*Recreational vehicle? Check.*

*250-foot-long driveway? Check.*

At a square footage of 6,000, our home offered plenty of space to grow our family. My wife took charge as *housewife*. She cooked and cleaned. She took care of our children, and she'd begun homeschooling them and a few children from our church. Most—if not all—roads led to our home; something was always going on. People were always visiting.

# THE JOURNEY TO AUTHENTICITY

The Black Church in America is known for praising, exalting, and honoring its pastors. I was elevated as a Man of God. I didn't want for anything; my church members took care of me as their "passah." My drivers took me to church services and special events. I was given fine clothes, and I had attendants to assist me in wearing this finery. I had more perks than I could ever use in this lifetime.

My life was a façade. This is why I cried.

After the floodgates opened, Lori left the room to alert Iyanla that I was in a state of emotional revelation. Through my tears, I heard Lori's heels gingerly clicking outside the door as she left to speak with Iyanla.

I felt a release and a new dimension of peace and freedom as Iyanla entered the room and knelt to embrace me. In that moment she was like a church mother with candy in her purse, each individually wrapped in brightly colored waxed paper, offering me a piece to ease my mind. Moments later Iyanla swaddled me. That rock bottom swaddling moment represented so much. I felt a much-desired sense of parental care and compassion.

Iyanla was both my undertaker and my midwife, gifting me with the death of my masked-self and the birth of my authenticity. I found my truth in rock bottom.

———————

## LifeWork: Rock Bottom

Over the years, people have asked me pointed questions about my life and marriage. None of their questions compare to what I have asked myself. *What am I thinking? Why do this now? How could I abandon my family? What about my marriage? What about my children? What about my parents and siblings? Am I hurting them? What about my church and everyone who believed in me? Had I used them, too?* I know I lied to myself and to those I love deeply. I needed to tell my truth. It was time to come out and live authentically.

I encourage you to take some time with these three *LifeWork* assignments. With all *LifeWork*, you get out of them what you put into them.

1. Where are you being faux-thentic? Why are you choosing to be fake? What can you do now to live differently tomorrow? Consider confessing your faux-thenticity to a trusted friend—or to a professional—who can serve as an accountability partner or a critical friend to support you being authentic.

2. I know I'm not the only one who's had a Rock Bottom experience. My Rock Bottom experience was with my sexuality and marriage. Your Rock Bottom moment might be with your health or money; it could be with your friendships or work relationships.

Are you living beyond your means? Are you going through the motions in your personal relationships? Do your friends know the *real* you? Take a moment to think about the power of having a Rock Bottom experience. Where could you grow or go if you were free? If you haven't had a Rock Bottom experience, what might be the reason?

3. Take thirty minutes to reflect on your life. Whether you are still in high school or days away from your retirement after a rewarding career, there's a chance you have more you wish to accomplish in life. What are two or three specific dreams or goals you wish to achieve? What can you do now to realize these dreams or goals within the next 90 days? Consider developing a short-term Vision Board and using creative visualization to manifest what you desire.

**Lifework Affirmation**
*I am brilliant beyond measure!*

# 3 BE COURAGEOUS

*Courage is the most important of all the virtues, because without courage you can't practice any other virtue consistently. You can practice any virtue erratically, but nothing consistently without courage.*
— Maya Angelou

For most of my adult life, I had been the perfect example of someone practicing virtues erratically. I wasn't honest, or steadfast, or patient—or any of the other values I claimed to hold dear—with any consistency. I wasn't courageous, my virtues were inconsistent. I now know telling people they're going to Hell is fueled by cowardice, which leads to fear. These emotions can attack one's courage.

I was feeling intense shame for things I thought as a child: *What's going on with me? Certain boys are attractive to me. Certain girls are attractive to me, too.* I was also feeling guilt for things I couldn't control: *Why is that man looking at me that way? Why do I get these random erections?*

I remember having a crush on my kindergarten teacher, Mrs. Covington. I was drawn to everything about her: The way she talked. How she entered the classroom. The way she curled her lip and tilted her head when she laughed. She had a silky, straight ponytail and brownish skin. And she made me feel special.

My crushes extended beyond my teacher to my classmates:

Gene Ellis, who would sit in front of me while Mrs. Covington held story time on the intricately designed carpet. Gene's curly afro always managed to block my optimal view of Mrs. Covington and the book she was reading. I didn't mind the obstruction; though, because he was cute.

Leslie Scott. Quick tempered (*Was it because older students teased him about his name?*). He shoved to get his way. The quintessential Bad Boy; yet, he never pushed me.

I can't forget Alice Anglin's big brown eyes that danced whenever the swing took her a little too high or after Rikki Chapman, the class clown, said something wildly funny. Ever the young fashionista, Alice's hair was in four immaculately twisted ponytails. She wore brightly colored dresses with matching tights and the prettiest pair of coordinating *Mary Jane* shoes.

I didn't think my attraction to boys and girls was either right or wrong. I didn't run home to tell anyone about my attraction. I didn't think it was strange. I didn't think it was good or bad. It just was. There wasn't an influence from anyone, one way or the other, to feel a certain way. My feelings were straight from the heart. They didn't feel weird, and I didn't feel weird about having them.

This was an impressionable moment in time, not just for me, but for most children. These defining moments are divinely intended. These events are not random—I believe nothing is random. Childhood was an amazing time and place. Not a care in the world. No overthinking. No self-judgement. No judging. No prejudice. No hate. No idea of racism. No idea of sexuality. Pure innocence. *Can we return to this innocence and purity again?*

---

Oftentimes, traditional church attitudes and teachings don't evoke courage, at least not from within. To me, courage is to be brave, bold, daring, and unflinching in the face of daunting fears. It is making and managing tough decisions. I've had moments when I thought I was courageous, but later I discovered I wasn't. It took me some time to share the next story. It's a delicate situation but one I hope will help bring healing to you and others.

My brother and I shared a single-wide trailer for a couple of years. We must've been around 21 at the time. My parents purchased the trailer from my aunt, and it was next door to our parents' home.

Living on our own was cool—even if we were just steps away from our parents. I enjoyed the privacy and the freedom. It allowed me to be *down low* well before the phrase became popular. I'd slip off to gay clubs in neighboring cities to explore that hidden part of me. What started as just weekend visits to clubs and other hot spots turned into outings many times a week. I loved it! Somehow, I was always awake and ready for church on Sunday morning, even if I partied or hooked up the night before.

During this time my nephew, Trevor, was staying with my parents next door in the "big house." He'd come over to visit me and my brother since it was cooler than hanging out with "paw-paw and granny." He adored us because it actually was cooler. We always had some game underway. One day, Trevor and I were roughhousing like we did often.

"Ladies and gentlemen! What a great upset! *Mitchell the Magnificent* has *Too Tough Trevor* in a headlock."

"It's looking bad for *Too Tough* . . . Oh no!"

"Mitch pins him down. One! Two! Thr—"

"Uncle, Mitch, Stop!"

I froze.

I jumped up.

We wrestled and play fought often. Sometimes I won; other times I let Trevor beat me. I'd pinned Trevor down that day, but this time he was on his back and with my legs wedged between his.

I felt confused.

I hadn't looked at my nephew in a sexual way—
and I wasn't starting to do so then.

I obsessed for days at the thought that there was
a possibility this situation *could have* crossed the line.
I questioned if this was my *demon* returning to
destroy my life.

I replayed the events in my head so often.

I wondered: *Had I actually crossed the line?*

I felt the best solution to combatting my demons
was to suppress my sexuality even more. No more
clubbing, no more house parties in Petersburg. No
masturbation. My life consisted of home, work, and
church.

Work. Church. Home.

Praying. Fasting.

Church. Home.

Work.

Praying.

Fasting.

I began to question my purpose, my calling, my
gifts, and God's love for me. I had been flirting
with starting a preaching ministry for so long.

*Will God kill me when I give in to being gay? How can I
still play the organ on Sundays? How can I still sing and
direct the choir? Why are people still moved, touched, and
blessed by my gifts? Why does God still use me after my
thoughts—and at times actions—with men were so sinful
just hours before?*

Negative thoughts sent me into a tailspin of
emotions and questions, blocking any action.

After some time, I retreated to confess my feelings at the only place I knew I could: the church. One night, I attended confession at my church. We decided to use the Prayer Circle time to free us from the shame of whatever past we'd created. I revealed my attraction to men and I recalled various gay sexual experiences. My nephew was in the Prayer Circle that night. And then, I apologized to him for the wrestling match I thought had gone wrong. The reality is that I hadn't done anything wrong; when he said, "Stop!" I did. I was reacting to society's less than favorable assumptions about gay men and young boys.

Looking back, I now see how we sometimes get a natural high from public confessions in church. I recall witnessing many pregnant teenagers shamed into apologizing to the entire congregation. I'm not sure if this was to teach the girl about sin or to make everyone feel better about *failing* the young lady. It rarely made the girl feel like a Child of God (boys were decidedly absent—they're never really required to publicly acknowledge their seminal role in bringing babies into the world. It's an awful double-standard, but I digress). We should stop to ask ourselves, who benefits from such confessions?

Years later, my nephew contacted me. He wanted to discuss the incident and his understanding of my apology. I hadn't recognized my nephew for who he was at that time—a young boy. It's possible my public confession was jarring. My nephew could've felt dumbfounded or embarrassed. Either of those would've closed him off to receiving my truth in that forum. Or maybe he wasn't ready to hear such vulnerability surrounded by church members. The key is I was stating *my truth*.

Mortified, I reflected on that night in the Prayer Circle. I thought I'd humbled myself and apologized. Obviously, that night was about my confession and not about him at all.

I was selfish.

Eventually, we met face-to-face to talk about the day we wrestled. As he recollected, I listened and realized I hadn't crossed a line. *What a weight off my spirit!*

My nephew taught me about courage that day. He confronted an uncomfortable situation and asked for clarity. To move forward, he needed a clear sense of things. His courageous retelling of the events of that day years ago calmed the fears I had about doing something wrong.

Part of my courage was admitting that my truth isn't the same as everyone else's truth. I had to admit it wasn't all about me and my assumed guilt. People think it's especially courageous to admit things in front of large groups of people. We unfairly associate true repentance with public shame. Oftentimes a public apology is about validating the offender. It's not about making true amends to the offended person.

I think it's harder to look someone in the eye, hold their hand, and apologize. Face-to-face. One-on-one. To apologize without the validation of the crowds takes true selflessness and courage. I am thankful to my nephew for teaching me this lesson about true courage. Too often we allow our emotions to fester and sit because we don't want to offend others or rock the boat. We must demand clear and acceptable explanations from others. It is not just our right; it's our responsibility as human beings.

———————

I reconnected with my nephew, Trevor, while driving to Wisconsin. I hadn't seen him in years and I excitedly awaited his arrival for breakfast. My nephew, his three adorable children, and I dined at a small cafe, reminiscing, laughing, and reconnecting. I ate the largest pancake in the world and marveled at the father Trevor had become. I'm so thankful for that moment created by courageous acts.

———————

## Life Work: Be Courageous

Maya Angelou couldn't have said it better, "Courage is the most important of all the virtues..." This is why it's my first Secret to Getting the Life You Desire. A tortoise cannot move forward without sticking its neck out. At the heart of courage is risk-taking. We must be tortoise-like in our quests to become who we desire. We must take risks if we seek to be courageous and live life free from cowardice. We must move boldly, even in the presence of fear.

I encourage you to take some time with these three *LifeWork* assignments. With all *LifeWork*, you get out of them what you put into them.

1. Reflect on the painful moments in your life and select one experience that remains unresolved (ideally, this is a pain point just below the surface that time hasn't healed). What courageous thing will you do now to start the healing process? What joyful moments are you missing because you haven't taken a stand, apologized, made a change, or forgiven? Who can assist you in moving forward?

2. To some people, values and beliefs are nothing more than guidelines offering parameters. To others, values and beliefs are confining and limiting; they curb creativity and demand compliance and conformity by boxing people in. What are some values and beliefs you find limiting? Which ones tend to box you in? I encourage you to reflect on the limiting values and beliefs and *LiveLifeLiv* beyond the box. What specific thing will you do now to live courageously?

3. If we aren't careful, we worry what people will say about our life decisions. Also, we'll compare our journey to the journeys of others. I've learned the grass *is* greener on the other side; it's because people are pumping gallons of water and are shoveling mounds of manure! Which parts of your life have you been comparing to the experiences of others? Have you compared your marriage, your children, your car, your income, your vacation, your looks, or more to others? How have such comparisons made you feel? What will you gain by courageously stopping the comparisons now?

**Lifework Affirmation**
*I am courageous!*

# 4 BE VULNERABLE

*What happens when people open their hearts?*
*They get better.*
— Haruki Murakami, *Norwegian Wood*

To be vulnerable is to be free, unencumbered by the perceptions and thoughts of others. It is to engage in reflective self-discovery and self-actualization. This engagement is often done in the midst of our own denials. To be vulnerable is to be open to a full range of emotions, feeling each one, in public and in private. It's also the willingness to receive support and guidance, without ego. Being vulnerable is something we must *grow through* on our journey to authenticity. True growth means we will be vulnerable many times throughout our lives.

There is a moment in the broadcast of *Iyanla's Fix My Life* when Iyanla suggested I preyed on Diamond. She accused me of using my ex-wife's situation as a single mother of three to take advantage of her. She hypothesized that I used Diamond's vulnerability as an unwed mother so I could have guilt-free affairs. I vehemently denied those accusations, and I soon realized nothing I could say at that moment would be received. I decided to wait until now to tell the rest of the story.

Many people have asked how Diamond and I met. *Did you two meet at church? Were y'all out clubbing? Did she catch your eye in the produce section at the grocery store?* She and I met the way so many of us do: a mutual friend introduced us over the phone. I fell for Diamond before I ever met her in person. She and I would chat about everyday life. I enjoyed talking to her about anything. Our conversations were easy and effortless. She seemed level-headed, full of wisdom, and I thought she was mature. I didn't think about her age—she was only 22—or that she had three very small children.

Not long after we were introduced, she took an extended weekend trip to attend her stepfather's retirement ceremony. I realized then I missed talking to her. I left at least three voicemail messages for her. Later on, she told me she just couldn't understand why I was *blowing up* her phone with so many calls. When I finally heard from her, I was overjoyed.

"I miss you," rushed from my mouth.
"Really?" she responded, half-amazed.

"I've gotten so used to talking to you...I can't wait to see you."

All this happened before we met in person. She lived in South Carolina and I was in Virginia. I was intrigued and began to pursue her with tenacity. After a few more days, I asked her to send me a picture. I'd only heard her voice. I hadn't seen a photograph of any sort. I must admit, the Prayer Warrior in me got to work:

*Father God, You said in Your Word You'd give us the desires of our heart. Well, Father God, You know my heart and You know I love all Your children, but please, Father God, don't send her to me in a five-ton package. In the matchless name of Jesus, I pray. Amen.*

Then I waited for her email. Diamond said she'd send the only picture she had. I opened her message shortly after it arrived. *Lord, have mercy!* Somebody could've bought me for a dollar and gotten back ninety-nine cents in change.

If I didn't know any better, I would've thought I was looking at something from a *JET Beauty of the Week* photoshoot. Diamond had on a two-piece swimsuit that caressed every curve of her beautiful body. She was leaning on a brick wall, gazing over her shoulders at the camera. Before I knew it, I was humming a classic song by *The Commodores.*

*BAW baw baw baw baw baw*
*Boom baw baw...*
*Aww, a Bric—*

I thanked her for sending the picture and I thanked God for answering my prayer. *Brick House*, indeed.

We arranged a face-to-face meeting for the following weekend. I drove to Sumter, South Carolina. We decided to meet in my hotel lobby that evening and then drive to Columbia, South Carolina for dinner. Once I arrived in Sumter, I let her know I was in town and zipped by the florist. I had to find *Birds-of-Paradise*. They were beautifully arranged and I knew Diamond would love them. I did the usual pre-date things hoping to calm the butterflies in my stomach. I got my car washed and I changed clothes. She called to let me know she was nearby—I wasn't the only one who was anxious!

She strolled into the hotel lobby; the picture had hidden more of her beauty than I thought. Her jeans, halter top, and sandals were casual and chic. We jumped into my car and peeled out of the lot bound for Columbia. We held hands the *entire* trip, which was a feat in a five-speed stick-shift car.

I was determined to start our courtship with honesty. I told her about my experiences with men. I assured her I'd given up that part of me; I told her she had nothing to worry about. I loved her, and she loved me. The love we shared, and my pleas to God, would keep the gay in me at bay. It wasn't long before my sermons turned up the volume against gay, lesbian, bisexual, and transgendered people. I preached that all of them were an abomination, and God wouldn't have anything to do with such sinners. I put her at ease.

I married a woman with three children and became a husband and a father overnight. I felt validated and rewarded as a new father. It was a seamless shift because my parents were great role models for what it meant to care for a family. Our family was young; our boys were two years old, one year old, and nine months old when Diamond and I met. I felt gratified. I was blessed by God. I'd been given this special assignment to raise my sons and commit to my new wife.

I define marriage differently than almost everyone I know. I believe marriage begins when two consenting adults have intercourse. I remember when Diamond and I made love in August 2004. Shortly thereafter, I told my congregation about my marriage beliefs. I'm sure some wondered privately; however, they were visibly receptive of my thinking. What I now know is that my marriage message was the first step I made in transforming my mind and shifting my consciousness. A year later, Diamond and I received our license and got married according to the laws of the land—just as I told my congregation we would.

Once we married, more children quickly arrived. Our family grew to include Karyn, Kendall, Kourtney, Karl, Kenyan, and Kasey. Everything was in warp-speed. I had a new life with a woman and children. My ministry had recently merged with another church and it continued growing. We were renovating my bachelor pad into something suitable for a growing family. Life was good, and it was unfolding faster than we could envision.

As the church grew, so did our successes. We moved to a bigger house, and things were on the right track. Soon, with more money came more problems. I did what many of us do when we face challenges—I returned to something I thought I had let go. That's when I realized Diamond and I had shielded parts of our true selves at the beginning of our marriage. Things began to unravel. My attraction to men was still there, just below the surface. Diamond and I found ourselves looking outside our marriage for intimacy and comfort.

Despite challenges in my marriage, I broadened my spiritual horizons. I considered myself a student of the Word. I began to study *The Bible* more diligently on my own and through the writings of others, independent of the church. I'd break down each word in a verse using *Strong's Concordance*. I wanted to get back to the original meaning of the scripture (I thank Carlton Pearson and one of my brothers for this awareness).

The things I learned shook the foundation of my beliefs, and I was initially afraid to share this new information with my church. I learned the four names of God: *Yahweh, Jehovah, Elohim,* and *Elohem.* These were not different names for the same God as I'd been taught through the years. These were different gods! I grew up Baptist; this new way of seeing God was foreign and unlike anything I'd learned.

I had to steady myself each time I learned something new. I learned that Abraham was a Hebrew; I hadn't been taught this. I learned he was the father of God's chosen people, the Jews. Time would dictate that I'd require all leaders in our church to use *Yahweh* when referring to the name of God.

*Had I gone too far? Was I looking too deeply? What else had I learned that was wrong?*

I changed the format of our Sunday services to allow questions after my sermons. We began to study the history of *The Bible*. I soon asked our members to buy *Strong's Concordance* and encouraged them to unravel the Scriptures for themselves. I removed religious barriers and upset generational control. I wanted them to "Study to shew thyself approved unto God" II Timothy 2:15.

The scriptures were no longer the same for those who did the work. The most devastating blow came from discussing Heaven and Hell. I'd spent days researching the concepts. The more I learned about *The Bible*, the more I sought to liberate others by giving them the tools I'd used to unlearn and learn.

Church wasn't the same after I debunked the idea of Hell being an actual place. Everyone's confusion was evident. People began to leave our church. Some told me about their decision, while others quietly left. Even my parents left. What was chaotic and confusing to them was liberating and clear to me. *Why can't they see what I see? How do I get them to live a full life free from Hell fire?*

The church crumbled and emptied. By November, our accounts were dry and I no longer received a salary. *Was I crazy? Why are they leaving?* I believe I now understand why people left: Fear.

My marriage dissolved because I accepted myself as a same-gender loving man. I expanded my thinking about Christianity through studying and questioning. I felt vulnerable and very much alive. Embracing and accepting my sexuality took me down a different path.

---

Diamond and I were in the master bedroom. It was a Sunday morning. Diamond was still recovering from oral surgery. I worried about her pushing herself to be *on* as the First Lady of our church. While it isn't a paying position, the First Lady's work complements the work of the pastor. She decided she'd stay home on the mend.

This particular day, I lay next to Diamond while I scrolled through my *Facebook* timeline. *Facebook* and other forms of social media are hotbeds of opinions and ideas. These days, many of us sit in front of our screens banging out fiery responses. Some of our comments uplift; other comments tear down.

My niece popped up on my *Facebook* timeline. She was outing a schoolmate who was following her around campus. I figured she had a crush on my niece. Maybe, I thought, my niece didn't want anyone to assume the interest was mutual. I read a few more postings from my niece and saw the beginnings of a *Facebook* assassination. It didn't matter if the girl identified as lesbian. What mattered was the treatment she received at the hands of my loved one. Before I knew it, I wrote in defense of my niece's schoolmate.

Timing is everything, and Diamond didn't miss the opportunity to share something that had been on her mind.

"At the rate you're going, Mitchell, either you're no longer going to believe that Hell exists," she paused, "or you're going to believe that God wouldn't condemn or punish homosexuality."

She let her wonderings sit with me for a moment and continued confidently, "If you reach either of those, would you go back to it?"

I already knew which *it* she was speaking about.

"Probably so," I answered within seconds.

I gazed out on the water; she looked at the ceiling.

*What was she thinking?*

*What emotion had I jostled?*

We sat in silence and wept.

This wasn't how I'd thought my day would unfold. I hadn't planned on being direct and honest about my thinking.

I knew my marriage was over.

*What would I do? We have five kids.*

*This house. These cars.*

*This life.*

I was late for church.

Diamond stayed in the bed, pondering.

I could hear my mama's mantra ringing in my ears, "Never let them see you sweat!" as I loaded the kids in the car. I had to hold my head at just the right angle to keep my children from catching me cry. I felt immense joy *and* pain. I didn't want to admit the strange sense of freedom I felt overcome me.

I rushed over to hug my dad when I arrived at church. I instantly felt better. After service, I gave our nanny money to take the children somewhere, anywhere. She loaded them into my *Escalade*, and I took her car. I wanted to get home to have some Think Time with Diamond.

Diamond was still in bed when I arrived. I stood in the doorway for a moment and then sat on the floor. At first, I noticed the patterns on the ceiling. I scanned the photographs around the room. I didn't know where to start, but I knew I had to be vulnerable and risk it all to live my life authentically.

Once we started, Diamond and I talked for hours uninterrupted. I was so engaged in our heart-felt conversation, I forgot to remove my coat and shoes. Neither of us moved.

As darkness engulfed our picturesque neighborhood; we didn't bother with lamps and nightlights. We sat in the knowing comfort of darkness. People fear darkness. Darkness is often described as evil. There is an unease associated with darkness. We mustn't forget the power of darkness, however. It is the place of purpose. Darkness is also symbolic of the womb and birth. I sensed our forthcoming debut as new creations. I didn't know what would come of it, but I knew this darkness was pregnant with possibility. We reflected on our marriage and the decisions we'd made. We talked about our lives and the ways we had grown. We discussed our children and our hopes for them. We wondered about our families and how they would receive the news. *Which kinfolk would need consoling? Who might be applauding, or otherwise celebrating?* The darkness willingly gave us protection and urged us to be vulnerable.

We talked through the night, finally drifting off to sleep. I continued puzzling through our conversations as I slept: *Did we just talk about all that? Are we really growing apart? What about our children? Will Diamond be OK? Am I dreaming?* We talked for several more days and mapped out a plan for telling our children.

Nothing prepares parents to tell their children about divorce. Nothing prepares children for the loss of innocence at that moment. Diamond and I gathered our children to tell them about our decision. They sensed this wasn't the typical meeting to announce our family vacation destination. Mommy and Daddy weren't launching an investigation into who'd really broken a dinner plate and hastily glued it back together, only to have it split into pieces.

JONES

The pain on their faces and the heartache in their voices are as fresh and cutting to me today as they were back then.

Kendall wondered, "Daddy, who's gonna protect us if someone breaks in the house?"

Karl bounced downstairs to tell the nanny. Kasey was too young to know what was happening. He curled up to his brother with wide eyes.

Kendall, Kourtney, and Kenyan cried.

Diamond and I cried. Heartbreak was seeping throughout our home.

It all changed in an instant. *What about commitment? What about family? What about love?*

Diamond and I announced our separation to our family and friends by email. December 2009 was one gut-wrenching month!

---

My relationship with Diamond was organic and real. It wasn't a sham marriage; I wasn't searching for a *beard*. If I wanted a beard—a person who knowingly or unknowingly conceals a person's sexual orientation—I wouldn't need to look any further than my own town. I didn't need to venture states away to find a woman to marry me as a coverup. I saw Diamond as the piece missing from my life. I believed she would sustain me for the rest of my life.

When Iyanla pressed my thinking and asked if it were possible I'd subconsciously exploited Diamond's position, I remembered who I was back then. And as much as I didn't like the sound and feel of it, I realized there was some truth to Iyanla's beliefs about my actions. Admitting this was tough, but I chose to be vulnerable.

---

### LifeWork: Be Vulnerable

True vulnerability is not carrying shame after you lose it all. It's sacrificing material things for peace of mind and freedom—be it the expense of a divorce, the loss of friends or community. It's going from this year's *Escalade* to a late model used car. It's going from a 6,000 square foot house to a one-bedroom apartment. It's being unafraid of the whispers in the background. It's knowing the saying, "The bigger they are, the harder they fall," won't define you as a person. Being vulnerable was telling my wife I am attracted to men. Being vulnerable is having my children's perception of me change. It's being willing to accept their new perception, whatever it is. There is a divine gracefulness in being vulnerable. Vulnerability is the true meaning of *Surrendering All.*

I encourage you to take some time with these three *LifeWork* assignments. With all *LifeWork*, you get out of them what you put into them.

1. We have been taught to *woman* or *man* up; lest someone sees us as weak and vulnerable. There is power in vulnerability. This goes

against everything many of us have been taught since childhood. What could you gain by being vulnerable?

2. Many times, we harden ourselves because we don't feel safe enough to be vulnerable. We worry that what we say will be used against us. "A friend is someone who knows enough about you to destroy you but would never do so." If you haven't been vulnerable, who in your life represents a safe space for you to practice being vulnerable? Which friend can you count on to create a space to safely nurture your vulnerability?

3. Being vulnerable is having the courage to stand where you are and the faith to know things will get better. Walking away is not a problem—walking away and having learned nothing is a problem. Being vulnerable is knowing when to walk away with learning. What will you do now to be vulnerable? What learning will you take with you?

**Lifework Affirmation**
*I am graciously vulnerable!*

# 5 BE STEADFAST

*Lord, give me firmness without hardness, steadfastness*
*without dogmatism, love without weakness.*
— Jim Elliot

The journey to authenticity is just that, a journey.
You can't just wake up one morning and say, "Hey,
I'm going to clean up all my mess," and expect to
be free and clear by lunchtime. When you've had
years of faux-thentic living, it takes time. It just
doesn't happen instantly. Most of the time we need
to get out of our own way and take the first step on
our journey to authenticity.

Books like *The Journey to Authenticity* are filled
with practical, transformative tips suggesting who
you must *be* to *do* what you must do to *have* the life
you desire. We must take what we read and apply it
to our lives. Life coaches can meet with us week
after week and month after month to plan the life

we desire; yet, we still have work only we can do. We must do this part alone if we seek more than quick fixes and if we desire sustained growth.

Our wives and husbands, parents and coworkers, partners and children shouldn't do this work for us. You mustn't rely on your bae, sugar plum, or boo; your play aunt, Uncle Ray Ray, or baby daddy. They can't do our work because it won't have any meaning for us. If they do this work, it will always be their work and not ours. We must be resolute, firm, and unwavering. We must be steadfast.

———

After choosing to leave my marriage in December 2009, I remained in our house until February 2010. Then I decided to move in with my best friend and her family. They had a basement apartment with a separate entrance and access to the main floor. I figured downsizing would give me time and space to rethink my life.

One evening, I remembered a guy from my past. He was my first love. I was only 18 when he entered my life and touched my body and soul in ways I hadn't experienced before. I thought it would be good to reconnect with Mikel then. I remember the night we met: it was a blistering summer evening, and Mikel was dancing. He had a confident sexiness about his moves. I couldn't resist him and I also couldn't approach him. Thankfully, a dear friend saw me looking at him and introduced me to Mikel.

Mikel and I got to know each other and decided to date exclusively. I loved the time we shared. Our conversations. Our hugs. Our kisses. Our lazy afternoons and eventful nights together. We enjoyed these moments of bliss for a few months until Mikel pressed me to be authentic. That day he ended our relationship.

"I love you, but you aren't free. You're afraid to be yourself. I want someone who will be true to himself...and you aren't willing."

Back then I didn't understand where he was coming from.

*Who does he think he is? I know who I am! I ain't scared to be me. I only fear God.*

I wasn't ready then. I didn't know that I didn't know what I didn't know. After my separation, it was a new day. I'd grown up and I'd changed things in my life since then. I was finally ready for Mikel! I just had to track him down.

Finding Mikel wasn't much of a challenge. Social media and the Internet have made searching for friends and loved ones easy. I reached out to Mikel and filled him in on my journey. I talked about my marriage and the separation. I shared pictures of my children and gushed about the joys of fatherhood. He talked about his life and told me he was single. I kept it together on the outside, but inside I was doing a Holy Ghost shout and speaking in tongues!

We didn't waste any time reconnecting. It was like picking up from where we left off in the 90s. We talked each day. Eventually, we spent weekends together. Mikel and a friend helped me clear out the home I'd recently shared with my wife. The plan was to move into my friend's basement; however, with each item we tossed or packed, Mikel and I discussed the advantages and disadvantages of that move. We agreed the cost and the commute didn't make sense. We also agreed to live together!

I really didn't need much convincing to respectfully turn down my friend's offer for a living space and move in with my first love. The reconnection was all I imagined it would be and more. We'd talk for hours unaware of the time. Mikel and I made use of *every* bed in his three-bedroom home. When we went out to eat or shop or see a game, people figured we were two straight guys enjoying a *bromance* moment. They only had to stare a few seconds longer to notice how we looked at each other or the way we embraced to know we were more than friends. The energy between us was amazing. I was living my fairytale.

And as fast as my fairytale began, it ended. One night, I returned home to find our home silent. I looked around for Mikel. At first, I thought he was playing a game that would have us testing out the new mattress.

*He certainly knows how to keep the home fire burning!*

I searched everywhere. This wasn't a game. He wasn't home. Then I noticed he'd left his cellular phone behind. He was always joined at the hip to that thing. I began to worry; it was a dreadful night. Mikel came home around 8:00 the next morning. I learned so much that day. Mikel had been addicted to drugs and in my search for a relationship, I'd missed the signs. His challenge with drugs shifted his thinking and affected his decision-making. We were four months into our renewed relationship and he was having an emotional affair with a guy he'd met through social media. I was hurt and confused.

*How could I miss the signs? Am I not worthy of love? What must I do?*

After breaking up with Mikel, I moved in with my parents. Home was a much-needed oasis. I took the time to reflect and heal. I also had time to save money and rebuild my credit after the separation. It's always a challenge returning home. I had to remember rules and expectations I'd long forgotten. It was a stretch, but I made it work. It had to work.

I eventually found a place in Newport News, Virginia: a 1,600 square foot condominium with three bedrooms and an open kitchen and living area. I am thankful the landlord heard my story and gave me a chance to rent from him. I moved into my place in January 2011. I already had my living room squared away; I just needed to find everything else for my bachelor pad. *Craigslist* became my furniture-finding friend.

My true challenge was returning to an empty house every day. Gone were the sounds of a home filled with family. I didn't come home to a light left on accidentally by one of my children or purposely by my wife. The washer and dryer weren't humming away making light the work of cleaning our clothes. No flickering television, no sounds from the radio. No laughter. No hugs. No wife or children to welcome me home or to ask about my day. I was home alone.

I'd waited until I was 30 before I decided I'd get married because I really enjoyed being single. Once I married Diamond, I took on the role of father and willingly gave up the single life to be a part of something greater. I loved so much about married life and I loved being a father. Being there at 39 after a few relationships and marrying Diamond, I realized that was the first time I was alone. From the time I was conceived, I was with my twin. I'd grown up surrounded by a large family. I was never alone until then.

I wasn't lonely; I was just in a place where the next thing to do wasn't already waiting for me. I began to question my purpose and identity. Along with the absence of the trappings of a family, I no longer had church responsibilities.

*Who was I without the robe? What would I become without the church?*

I didn't have board meetings and funerals, weddings and ministerial alliance events. I didn't need to plan for anything. The silence was painful. The solitude became painful. I didn't want to deal with knowing myself separate from everything and everyone else. My identity was always tied to someone or something else. I'd wanted to admit it, but it was challenging.

Not only did *Craigslist* help me fill up my home with furniture, I soon turned to it to soothe me by filling the gigantic void I felt. Although I told myself I was seeking companionship, what I usually found was hot sex. Sure, I found guys who enjoyed chatting online without the slightest thought of physical intimacy. I ventured to bars with some of them; I even spent sex-less quality time with them in their homes or mine. Some days I found someone I could meet; other days I was unsuccessful. I spent many hours online searching for people to make me whole.

I needed a strong wake-up call and I got one: a sexually transmitted infection. I was swimming in an ocean of irony. I'd begun a journey of spiritual and self-discovery. Along the way, I'd reframed my understanding of God, the concept of Hell, and my purpose. I'd experienced the downfall of my marriage and the decimation of my church. I'd stopped the lying and deception. I was looking at life and spirituality afresh. I should've been free!

I was on the verge of a new beginning and had lots of new learning. Somehow, though, all this knowledge wasn't doing me a bit of good. I had *backslid* into my old ways. I wasn't ready to use this new knowledge to transform my life. Random sexual encounters with people who really weren't invested in my well-being had taken priority. God had given me the gift of silence and solitude, and I was squandering it. I'd taken the easy path and reverted to old patterns.

Eventually, I decided to be steadfast and unmovable. I changed my focus; I decided to get to know me. I chose to sit with myself to learn as much as possible about me. I loved on myself. It felt great to embrace me. I returned to the gym and worked out with diligence. Because I'd learned the essence of wellness, I knew exercising alone wasn't enough. I changed my eating habits and loved my body with self-care. I began to enjoy me and the simple discoveries and rediscoveries about life. After spending quality time with myself, I focused on being the best father possible to my children.

I have become steadfast in living an authentic life. I can be a same-gender loving man without being on the prowl for meaningless, disconnected sex. Let me be clear, I'm not sex shaming. Sex is an amazing gift. I just choose to be purposeful in my sexual experiences. I choose to be safe, tenacious, and steadfast. This secret helped me nurture meaningful connections and do my *LifeWork* to become the man I'm destined to be. I've become comfortable with me, understanding of who I am, and clear about my contribution to the world.

---

### LifeWork: Be Steadfast

I stumbled upon this insightful quotation not long ago, "I survived because the fire within me burned brighter than the fire around me." The fire within me needed to be stoked. This fire fueled my next successful move, which fueled the next successful move, and so on. Failure becomes short-lived when this fire within burns brightly. This fire—which represents Steadfast—enabled me to find another way to make things work. This fire propelled me when critics were hard at work attacking my views and ideas.

I encourage you to take some time with these three *LifeWork* assignments. With all *LifeWork*, you get out of them what you put into them.

1. Some people use *steadfast* and *stubborn* interchangeably; I do not. While they may be two sides of the same coin, being steadfast is really about being attentive, determined, focused, and purposeful. Where aren't you being steadfast? Why are you choosing to give up? What can you do now to be steadfast?

2. Scholar Joseph Campbell encouraged us to follow our bliss. I believe we must be relentless in our pursuits. Think of one dream you have not realized. Take a few moments now to brainstorm specific steps you will take to exercise the secret of being steadfast. Share your plan with a trusted friend and schedule a ten-minute check-in

meeting for a few months from now to update her on your progress.

3. If you've developed a short-term Vision Board, take at least thirty minutes to reflect on where you are right now. I believe dreamers are only guaranteed sleep; therefore, I strive to be active. How are you being steadfast and active now in pursuit of the life you desire?

**Lifework Affirmation**
*I am steadfast!*

# 6 BE FORGIVING

*To forgive is to set a prisoner free and discover*
*that the prisoner was you.*
— Louis B. Smedes, *The Art of Forgiving*

I have learned that holding on to a negative
situation, or the feeling someone has mistreated me,
is a magnificent way to block my blessings. Holding
on to that moment or that person—and not
forgiving—prevents us from growing and *growing*
*through*. If we are to surpass our old selves and
*LiveLifeLiv*, we must forgive others and ourselves.

When Diamond and I were dating, I told her
about my past. I explained my sexual encounters
with men, and I discussed what I saw then as my
deliverance from homosexuality. What I hadn't
revealed were my infidelities. I'd cheated on
Diamond with five men. I admitted this during the
taping of *Fix My Life*.

Iyanla pressed me for details, "Book, chapter, and verse. Book, chapter, and verse."

I wrestled with what to say to Diamond and Iyanla. I was harboring a spirit of unforgiveness. I was holding on to it as if my life depended on it—and it *didn't*. I'd shared my infidelities by that point in the show; nothing remained hidden about me being unfaithful. I'd had affairs and encounters with men during our marriage; I'd confessed them. I was still trying to defend myself by engaging in a tit-for-tat game, though. I kept thinking about Diamond's affair. I'd kept quiet for so long; then I blurted out, "She cheated, too!"

"He *thought* I did," Diamond retorted.

And everyone moved on, but I couldn't get it out of my head.

———

Sometime in 2008, Diamond traveled to South Carolina to take care of a relative who'd been found at home unresponsive. Money had gotten pretty tight for us; I'd given Diamond just enough for a two-night hotel stay. I was thankful she could be there to support family. Diamond stayed in the hotel a third night; I knew neither of us had the money to do so. When I asked about the third night she said her cousin paid for the extra night.

The next morning I woke up with Diamond's cousin on my mind. It was such a thoughtful thing for him to do for us. I called and got his voicemail.

"Billy D! This is Mitchell. Thanks for taking care of that extra night at the hotel. We can always count on you. 'preciate it, man, be blessed."

I think you have to let people know when you appreciate something they've done. It only takes a few seconds to express gratitude. Satisfied I'd completed another thing on my To Do List, I looked in on the kids and checked the mailbox. Just as I opened the third piece of junk mail, my phone rang.

"Hey, hey, Billy D! Man, I wanna tha—"

"Mitch," he said, "I don't know what's up, but I ain't pay for no extra night at the Hampton."

"Wow!"

"Look, I keep outta grown people's business. I dunno what Di up to, but Imma stay outta it."

For whatever reason, I called another family member and got a similar response. Diamond was there for a visit, and she'd stayed at the hotel. Everyone was confused by my call. None of it made sense to me, but I figured Diamond would clear it all up when she got home. The next night she returned and said nothing about the hotel stay. I didn't bring it up. I certainly didn't want to argue on her first night home.

We were between homes and living in a large *Winnebago*. Things were cramped compared to our previous home; daily chores became complex. The combination washer and dryer unit in the *Winnebago* was so tiny it could've easily passed for the unit in my daughter's doll house. We had to wash daily or we'd get covered in an avalanche of dirty clothes. We tag-teamed on clothes washing duty and it was my time to tackle a mound of funkiness. I enjoyed this chore because it gave me time to reflect between the sorting, washing, drying, and folding.

I sat on the floor with a bushel of laundry, and I noticed a splash of color in the pile. I figured it was a new sports jersey or something.

*Hmmmm? What's this?*

I held the lingerie in the air, feeling its softness. I couldn't help but remember the first picture my wife sent me years before.

*I can definitely see Diamond in this.*

I was halfway down the path of planning a *private meeting* in our small bedroom when it dawned on me: I never required or asked Diamond to wear such things.

"Babe!" I shouted over the washing machine.

"Hey, babe, you gotta minute?" I lovingly asked.

I didn't want to let on that I'd done a 180 in my thinking. I'd gone from lustful longings to wondering about my wife's time away. *She did have a spring in her step.*

"Yeah, what's up?"

I put the pink lingerie on display. Trimmed in brown. Cut with precision.

*Snap out of it, Mitchell Jones!*

I could definitely see Diamond wearing it...briefly.

*Focus!*

"What's up with this?" I asked.

"Oh, Mitch, you remember when we had Angel's bridal party and the girls went shopping, don't you? Well, I bought it then. She's getting married! Everybody was buying lingerie. I had to buy something, too! You like it?"

*See, Mitchell, she had a reason to buy it...case closed.*

I tried to let it go, but her story kept pulling me back. It didn't sit well with me. I thought about her story and switched into Private Eye mode. I tracked down the tools of the trade and began my own investigation. I needed answers. I sought the truth.

*Can you handle the truth, Mitchell? Whenever you start searching, you'll find everything you're searching for.*

I requested detailed cellular phone bills. I installed stealth software on our computer. This software allowed me to see every keystroke made and every website visited.

After a few weeks of researching and investigating, I reached a conclusion and closed the case. I decided I'd wait a while; I needed more time to process what I'd discovered.

*...this is why they say curiosity killed the cat...*

Diamond and I went to a marriage seminar in Maryland the following week. We shared a lot and learned a lot. I began to ask her questions on the road trip home—two *looooong* hours. I wanted to give her a chance to come clean. The irony hadn't escaped me. I'd amassed mounds of information about her and was conveniently hiding my own dirt. We talked, but we didn't dig deeply enough. I couldn't wait to get home to show my evidence.

"I dunno where to start, babe, take a look at this..."

I gave her the cellular phone records.

"And this," I said without emotion.

Her eyes widened as she read the first email message.

"Ummm, and, umm, this."

The stealth software had worked its magic. She glanced at chat conversations.

*I gotcha.*

There's always pain and frustration before healing. For all my bravado, nothing had prepared me for the emotional affair I uncovered. We seasoned the air with a flavorful selection of *choice* words. She was so upset I'd spied into her life.

*'Where's the trust?' you ask?*

I was hurt that she'd attempted to *step out* on our marriage.

Diamond confessed to meeting someone from her hometown. They'd met at a funeral and had found each other attractive. She admitted she'd gone to the hotel to hook up with him.

"Mitchell," she paused, "Nothing happened. He couldn't get an erection...and by then I knew it was wrong."

Sex or not, touching or not, I was angry with Diamond. She asked for forgiveness for getting emotionally entangled with another man. I apologized for snooping around. We forgave each other; then we renewed our commitment to our marriage. I silently recommitted and resolved to end all intimate contact with guys. Of course, Diamond still had no idea what I was hiding.

When we point a finger at someone else, three fingers are pointing back at us. I put Diamond through Hell over her emotional affair with one person; yet, I'd said nothing about the five affairs I'd had with men. I met three of them online through *Craigslist*. Two were strangers to me and meant nothing more than a quick fix to whatever I was feeling at the moment. One was a listening ear in the aftermath of a heated argument. The other two men were relationships with the associated emotions and drama.

The two strangers were stereotypical *one-night stands*. These businessmen were in town for a day or two. They were curious and wanted to *play* with another man while *wifey* was home alone. I didn't want to know their real names; they never asked for mine.

Although Wade lived almost an hour away, somehow we ran into each other the night Diamond and I argued about her emotional affair. Our chemistry was electric, so I confided in him. I felt safe unloading all my troubles. And then we had great sex, the kind that eases your mind and curls your toes.

I met Gianni at a small hardware store in Virginia. I'd stopped by to find some painting materials and supplies. I saw him within seconds of entering the store. Tall and thinly built, Gianni's wavy hair was pulled back into a thick ponytail. A thick tuft of black hair poked through the V of his form-fitting sweater. His rugged boots accentuated the pair of *Levi's* he'd managed to pour himself into. I could count the change in his front, left pocket: *Twenty-five. Fifty. Sixty. Seventy. Seventy-five. Seventy-eight cents.*

He caught me counting his change, and we exchanged muted smiles. By the time I got to the cash register, I'd built up the courage.

"Look, I don't mean to be rude. I don't wanna freak you out. Would you like my number?"

*Dang, that was easy.*

And just like that, we connected. Since he lived only 15 minutes from our house, I'd stop by on my way home from meetings, rehearsals, and Bible study. I fell for Gianni; he was a proud Italian who exposed me to his culture. He spoke in Italian whenever we made love, and he talked to his dog in Italian!

After Diamond and I ended our relationship, I reached out to Gianni. It was yet another failed attempt to rekindle the past. It took me only three visits to discover that Gianni was struggling with alcoholism. With all I'd been going through in the aftermath of losing my family and my church, I decided I didn't want to add that experience to mine.

Renewing your license is typically uneventful. Take a number. Sit down. Sign some forms. Stay behind the line. See an agent. Take a new photo. Keep it moving. Tomás upset my plans and suddenly made renewing my license a party! He sauntered in with bubbling machismo. His *Timberlands* cradled the hem of his paint-spattered jeans.

*Dang, he's got at least ninety-five cents in that right pocket.*

His ruddy tan was mesmerizing; his pink lips inviting. I couldn't get his attention, but I knew I wanted to get to know him. I went to my car and scribbled my number on a scrap of paper. Then I waited for him outside.

"Excuse me," I caught his attention and saw his piercing eyes, "I'm Mitchell, and I gotta tell you, you're a beautiful man." I was forward.

He flashed a megawatt smile, "Thank you!"

His subtle accent had Spanish undertones.

"Here's my number. Give me a call. We can hang out. Grab a bite eat. You know, just chill."

Months went by before he called. I figured he wasn't gay or he wasn't interested. He'd moved and while unpacking and organizing his belongings, the scrap of paper fell from its hiding place.

"Man, I looked and looked for your number."

"I'm glad you found it!"

"Me, too!"

He knew about my wife and children and seemed to be cool with it all. He was almost two hours away. It was a scheduling nightmare at times, but we managed to see each other often. Over the months, I fell in love with him. I surprised him on his birthday. I took him to our home. I'd mapped out the visit to ensure no one would be there. It would be his first—and last—time there.

"You have a beautiful home, Mitchell. And you have a beautiful wife and children."

"Awww, thanks!"

"I love you."

"I love you, too!"

"I-I-I can't see you anymore."

*I can't breathe. Where has all the air gone? What's happening?*

Tomás, for all his masculine pride, had fallen in love with me. I thought I'd been the only one. He desired a long-term, same-gender loving relationship and he knew I couldn't give him what he desired. It was a long ride to his place and an even longer ride back home. I think being in my home and seeing pictures of my family made Tomás realize this truth.

I found Tomás on *Facebook* after Diamond and I ended our marriage. I told him I still cared for him, and I apologized for the way things ended with us. He told me he'd returned home to Mexico. I thought about visiting him. It didn't happen. He died that July. I was devastated. I remembered his smile and the times we shared. I wondered about a future with him:

*Had I missed out on the love of my life? What could we have accomplished together? Would our future have been as bright as we'd imagined? Would I find true happiness?*

Simple things can take us back in time: The smell of a favorite dish, the sights and sounds of a whimpering child, a look of anguish from the hero in a film, a touch on the shoulder. Our senses transport us to other related events. I found myself having a *Tonight-is-the-Night* à la Betty Wright moment and remembered my *very first time*.

I didn't have my first physical experience with a boy until I was maybe ten or eleven. I was at his house playing as we did throughout the summer. One hot afternoon we got our hands on a well-read copy of *Playboy* Magazine. We sneaked upstairs. My friend had the *Playboy* tucked in his pants in the small of his back. We gently closed the bedroom door. *Safe!*

He had an old-fashioned bed, not the kind I'd expect a boy to have had. It was a solidly built four-poster that had put in some service. We propped ourselves up with our elbows as we nervously flipped page by page. Large brown breasts greeted us, and we responded only as little boys could: we got erections.

As young as I was, I knew exactly what an erection was and what it could produce. I hadn't been taught about my body or sex; yet, none of that stopped me from self-exploration. I'd discovered masturbation. I was fascinated by my ability to please myself and was more than curious about the sticky liquid I could make with just the right touch.

There's nothing quite like a house without air conditioning at the apex of summer. We started to sweat as he made the first move. He grabbed my erection through my pants. It wasn't the same feeling I had grown to like. His grip felt strange. I was startled at first even though I'd wanted to touch him for months. Then it felt so good that I arched my back. We were still fully clothed, and he rubbed his growing penis against me. It throbbed. We kissed. I felt a tingle along my spine. I didn't wonder if this was right or wrong; I just knew it felt good. I didn't want him to stop.

"Take off your shorts."

I pulled them down, wondering briefly what we'd do if someone walked in on us. *Oh, we just playing.* Or, *we changing clothes.* No one ever did. He had experience and I was willing to learn. I did wonder, *Where'd he learn this?* We curled up and masturbated while thinking about *Playboy* Magazine and each other.

My friend and I had more experiences over the years of my youth. Back then, I didn't see our time together as sinful. Clearly, I'd missed all the *Adam and Steve's Amazingly Perilous Journey to Hell* sermons. If anything, what little guilt I had—if I had any—was because I was having premarital sex. Now *that* was a sin we'd heard about! I got over it and I lived a typical adolescence: I had girlfriends, I excelled in school, I played sports, and, of course, I experimented with more boys!

Over the years, my thinking shifted about my first sexual experience; I shrouded it in shame and guilt, and I attached potentially harmful feelings and emotions to my friend. We were both young boys who experimented with each other. I had to forgive myself and my friend if I really wanted to be free from my past.

I've wanted to beat myself up for the time I missed by not living authentically. I could've enjoyed my 20s and had a blast in my 30s; however, I had to stop thinking that way. My choices led me to a life with beautiful children to love. I know that sulking about the past won't get me anywhere. I had to forgive myself.

I had to forgive my wife for coping the best way she knew how. I had to understand that wherever we both were in consciousness was exactly the right place at that time. I had to forgive myself for being so hard on her. Maybe she suspected I wasn't able to give her what she desired, so she strayed emotionally.

I also had to learn to forgive the church for teaching me to disregard who I was. I had to understand that many people react out of fear of the unknown. I had to reconcile that some religious people accept the teachings of their trusted pastors at face value. And some don't have the time or ability to research years and years of misinformation. Oftentimes, people are just doing their best and know not what they do. I had to forgive them, as well.

———————

## LifeWork: Be Forgiving

Forgiveness and truth are necessary to repair our foundations and allow us to build upon them again. I had to be honest about my own transgressions to clear my mind. I had to be compassionate about other's faults before I could accept my own. I had to forgive myself if I were to continue working on being authentic.

I encourage you to take some time with these three *LifeWork* assignments. With all *LifeWork*, you get out of them what you put into them.

1. Take a moment to reflect on your past. Think of one moment or one person you haven't forgiven. If you are unable to forgive someone, you are unable to move forward. Who or what haven't you forgiven? Why haven't you forgiven? What is this accomplishing? How is it impacting your life now? Why are you allowing someone who wronged you so much power? What is awaiting you just on the other side of your forgiveness?

2. We all know at least one person who struggles to forgive. They haven't forgotten or forgiven something that happened five years ago, and when asked, they can't remember exactly why they're upset with the person or situation. They talk about the

people and situations and refuse to release them. Are you holding on to past hurts? Have you been unable to forgive? What will you do now to let go and forgive? I encourage you to write a letter to the person who wronged you, transporting yourself back in time and feeling all the emotions. Write all of this in the letter; then print it out, put it in an envelope, and seal it. Now, BURN it and release it. You can have a releasing ceremony at your home using your fireplace. You can build a small ceremonial fire outdoors (please be safe and have a fire extinguisher on hand, especially if you wrote a 30-page letter!). Whatever the case; release it and let it go.

3. "When I *hear* you say that, I feel *what*?!" asked Iyanla. "Oh, I'm just gonna slap the taste out yo mouth...Look at this woman and tell her the truth!" After I told the truth, I had to learn to forgive myself for hurting my ex-wife. Forgiving yourself is a gateway to forgiving others. Set aside at least 30 minutes to write down everything you've done that's been wrong, hurtful, mean-spirited, racist, sexist, and so on. Jot down all of the things you've done to judge others or make them out to be anything but a child of God. It's OK if you need to add more time to this process. Once you've written your list, stand in front of a mirror with your list, then look

at the first item on your list and say, "[say your name], I forgive you for [say the first item from your Forgiveness List]. You are forgiven. I am forgiven. We are forgiven." Repeat this until you have finished your list. Here's the deal, you'll need to speak your forgiveness like you really mean it. There's power in the spoken word.

**Lifework Affirmation**
*I am forgiving!*

# 7 BE GRATEFUL

*Do not spoil what you have by desiring what you have not; remember that what you now have was once among the things you only hoped for.*
— Epicurus

I remember the first time I studied the story of Job. It's a universal story, and I was taken by its poetic form. It's a familiar story of wealth, loss, and restoration. Who hasn't heard of long suffering, blameless Job? Job, who loved the Lord God, endured trial after trial at the hands of Satan. Some are quick to exclaim, "Oh, to be like Job!"

Life consists of mountains and valleys, moments of joyous triumph and life-altering instances of crushing defeat. At his lowest point—his valley experience—Job affirmed, "Naked came I out of my mother's womb, and naked shall I return thither: the Lord gave, and the Lord hath taken away; blessed be the name of the Lord." Job 1:21

*Oh, to be like Job!*

Admittedly, I see connections between and among Job, me, and many of my fellow pastors. Like Job, we strive to be "perfect and upright, [pastors who] feared God, and eschewed evil." Job 1:1. Job's wealth was measured in his possessions, "...seven thousand sheep, and three thousand camels, and five hundred yoke of oxen, and five hundred she asses, and a very great household..." Job 1:3. Our wealth is often measured by the size of our cathedrals, the kind of luxury cars we have, the locations of the homes we own, and the number of members we have on our unpurged membership rolls. Like Job, we are celebrated and honored.

Some pastors of large Black churches experience untold wealth and luxury. They create kingdoms with private jets and helicopters, many homes and cars, and a bevy of attendants to meet their every need. Although I didn't pastor a megachurch and we weren't raking in millions a year, my family and I had it all. At the height of our success, we owned luxury cars and a home on the water.

The most sought-after position in the *Royal Court of the Pastor* wasn't the praise team leader or the minister of music, even though these roles enrich the worship experience as the opening acts and the after-party to the headlining pastor's sermon. The most prized position is that of the pastor's attendant or armorbearer.

While there's great debate about the armorbearer and how the position is used, its advocates cite two supportive scriptures:

> "But Moses hands were heavy; and they took a stone, and put it under him, and he sat thereon; and Aaron and Hur stayed up his hands, the one on the one side, and the other on the other side; and his hands were steady until the going down of the sun."
> Exodus 17:12

> "And David came to Saul, and stood before him: and he loved him greatly; and he became his armorbearer." I Samuel 16:21

In essence, an armorbearer lovingly, willingly, and readily assists and supports a church leader in the operation of a ministry and in the realization of a God-purposed vision. Armorbearers support pastors so they may concentrate on ministering to people and delivering the Word of God.

I had a few armorbearers who took care of me as their shepherd. Sunday after Sunday, I'd descend the pulpit after passionate preaching. These moments are a state of ecstasy—a natural high—that is unmatched. I'd be drenched, soaked to the core. My armorbearers would spring into action, surrounding me as they whisked me into my office. Still savoring the presence of God, I'd stand as they carefully removed each piece of clothing. My robe and shoes. Then my shirt and t-shirt. Sometimes they'd change my pants, socks, and underwear because I was sweating profusely. They'd quickly clean me up and towel me off. They were efficient and I was often still in deep praise when they finished dressing me in clean, dry clothes.

We pastors grow accustomed to the privileges associated with our role. Some people are quick to judge, but it's easy to get used to the pampering. It happens beyond the church, whether the privileges are given to us or we pay for them. If you're a frequent flyer, you get to board your flight earlier than others, you may get to select a choice seat, or you may receive a complimentary upgrade to first class. Cruisers enjoy Platinum or Diamond access to special floors, events, and meals on cruise ships and at ports of call. I even know a friend who pays a few hundred dollars more for his family to skip to the front of the line at his favorite amusement park. And once you experience any of the privileges—once you've gotten a taste—life doesn't feel quite the same without them.

Once I realized there was more to God and my faith walk than I'd been told, I fed my spiritual growth with more and more information. As I expanded my horizons and grew my faith, I lost my pastoral privilege and luxury. And for all our talk about money being the root of all evil, try running a church without it! The more I preached about the oneness of humanity and the absence of Hell, the less we received in tithes and offerings. We had to reconsider our mortgages. We restructured salaries and allowances. We revisited and revamped many associations. Before long, I lost my marriage and my armorbearers.

How wonderful is our praise when we have everything we want and need. Our praise is overshadowed by our pain and we fall silent when we lose it all. Many have lost their minds after losing their possessions. We know a few stories of pastors who've killed themselves or disappeared from public life in the wake of loss and humiliation.

It's easy to grow comfortable with a staff attending to your every need. I'd grown accustomed to the constant presence of others. In the initial moments, I missed my armorbearers most. It's not uncommon for armorbearers and their pastors to develop close relationships. Armorbearers are privy to what happens when the organ playing ceases and the music stops. They observe their pastors as anointed *and* fully human. Like other pastors, I fully trusted my armorbearers. They were more than assistants; they became confidantes, and I missed their presence in my life.

I recalled the centuries-old letter Apostle Paul penned to the church of Philippi, "Not that I speak in respect of want: for I have learned, in whatsoever state I am, therewith to be content" Philippians 4:11. I knew I needed to enter this phase of my life differently, if I were to survive and thrive. I moved beyond the hurt and humiliation to find gratitude. I found praise and peace where others would sense hopelessness. I was grateful in the midst of the appearance of material lacking.

I took long walks and thought about my life. I had to face my new reality: my finances were in shambles. This didn't stand out until I saw my finances in writing. Over 90% of my members left our church. I'd lost 100% of my salary. Our home and luxury cars were gone. I realized I had to be grateful. My needs were met; I had a place to sleep, clothes to wear, and food to eat. I'd found a good job to support my children and their mother. I began to live like so many of my church members.

Making ends meet took on new meaning for me. I'd have private praise breaks to thank God for giving me a challenge to grow through. I didn't have the latest BMW, but I did have reliable transportation. I didn't have a lakefront house, but I did have a clean, well-maintained and loving home where I found peace and healing. And I was alive to experience it all. I lived in peace and calm. These feelings only deepened when I rediscovered giving.

Like many church members do week after week, I blessed what I had and gave it away. I looked at all my clothes: dozens and dozens of suits, slacks, and shirts. I could go for months without wearing the same combination. I wanted to make a fresh start and I knew giving would be a double blessing. I stuffed most of my clothes inside my car; the trunk groaned with the overflow of my Sunday's best. I found a Substance Abuse Treatment Center and blessed others who were also starting anew.

I knew God wasn't upset with me, despite the whispers of others. *Be Grateful* wasn't an other-worldly principle, it became my *LifeWork*. Every day I expressed my gratitude and gave. Some days I expressed appreciation for the rain. Other days I thanked God for insights into a problem I was attempting to solve. Some days I gave away hugs and smiles. Other days I gave the gift of compassion and another chance. Within months, I moved into a larger apartment with more bedrooms so my children would be comfortable.

I became appreciative of everything because each experience was preparing me for the next thing in my life. I'd reconnected with myself, and I fell in love with me. Even without the trappings of wealth (and even without my armorbearers), I knew every need would be met. I knew God would give me the desires of my heart. And although I wasn't sure of my next steps, I knew that all was—and would be—well: "For I know the thoughts that I think toward you, saith the LORD, thoughts of peace, and not of evil, to give you an expected end." Jeremiah 29:11

———————

## LifeWork: Be Grateful

I've heard of a high school in Greensboro, North Carolina, with a principal who partners with his students to host an annual *Sleep Out*. The *Sleep Out* is designed to help students learn about hunger and homelessness.

In the weeks leading up to the event, students collect cash and food donations. They donate the canned foods to a local pantry and they use the money to buy items for care packages to give to those who are experiencing homelessness. Warm gloves, scarves, wool socks, and toiletries are welcomed items to the children, women, and men. Speakers from local agencies talk about homelessness, providing the students with insights and resources. Students discover the science behind constructing shelters from discarded items and more. They learn about the disproportionate number of homeless veterans.

Armed with the knowledge they've gained and journals, the students spend the night outside in temperatures as low as 30 degrees. They wake up the next day with stories to tell. They are grateful. The *Sleep Out* is an experiential learning that will teach them for years to come.

I encourage you to take some time with these three *LifeWork* assignments. With all *LifeWork*, you get out of them what you put into them.

1. Reflect on your life—what has prevented you from demonstrating this secret? Go out and buy an old-fashioned journal or use the Notes feature of your smartphone and start a Gratitude Journal now. Each day or week, jot down eight things for which you are grateful.

Do your best to write different items without repeating. At least once a month reflect on your Gratitude Journal entries. What do you notice? Is your journal filled with thanksgiving for people or things? Do you express gratitude for events and experiences? If your gratitude is one-sided, what are other things for which you are grateful?

2. Set aside three minutes a couple of times a week to make a Gratitude Call to say how grateful you are for someone. Tell the person you want to share something and the only responses they can give you are "yes" and "thank you" . . . nothing else. Encourage them to pay it forward by calling other people. These are meant to be short calls. It should go something like this:

> *Hey Lora, how are you? I'm well. I started a gratitude journal a few days ago, and I've been thinking of folks who mean a lot to me. You're one of those people. I just want to take a minute to tell you something and you've gotta promise me you won't say anything other than yes or thank you. Lora, I am grateful for your friendship. You always tell me the truth, even when it hurts. I know you have my best interests at heart. You are giving. You are smart. You are creative. You are a visionary leader. I love how your mind works.*

*I love the way you take care of your family. I look up to you, and I'm a better person because I know you.*

3. There are times when we are unable to express our gratitude directly to someone. Perhaps the person you want to thank has died or is experiencing a life-altering health challenge like Alzheimer's Disease. Writing a letter to them is a great way to still express your feelings. You can write a letter to him, seal it in an envelope, and store it with your valuable possessions. You can write your letter on special water-soluble paper, say a prayer for her, and dissolve the letter in water. Take time now to write at least one letter.

### Lifework Affirmation
### *I am grateful!*

# 8 BE PATIENT

*A waiting person is a patient person. The word patience means the willingness to stay where we are and live the situation out to the full in the belief that something hidden there will manifest itself to us.*
— Henri J.M. Nouwen

I remember one of my cousins embracing Buddhism years ago. I was around 15 and she must've been at least 19. She was the coolest. My brother and I looked up to her. She lived in New York and did the big city things we dreamed of doing. She was open to exploring her spiritual connectedness. She used meditation and other Buddhist practices to elevate her consciousness.

"Nam-myoho-renge-kyo," she chanted, kneeling before a minimalist altar at her neighbor's home.

I didn't get it; *What was going on with my cousin?* She babysat for her neighbors and I just knew they were to blame for steering my cousin away from God. All I could think of as I barreled out of the room was getting struck by a heaven-sent lightning bolt. I knew God wasn't pleased with me for daring to consort with an idol worshipping demon—even if she was family! Back then I wrongly thought Buddhism was demonic; thus meditation was demonic. I believed it was an evil practice. It was against all I'd learned as a Christian.

Years later, I increased my awareness and shifted my thinking. I was soaking in so much information about myself and my connection to God and all humanity. It wasn't long before I discovered *Super Soul Sunday* on *OWN, The Oprah Winfrey Network*. I became an avid viewer of each episode. I found myself growing and learning so much during that time. They were just-in-time episodes; each topic seemed hand-crafted for me and my desires.

I connect a major shift in my thinking to a conversation Oprah Winfrey had with Russell Simmons about his book, *Success Through Stillness: Meditation Made Simple*. He and Oprah were chatting about meditation and how beneficial it was to his life and success. I bought the audiobook shortly thereafter. I raced through it, absorbing all Russell had to offer. I was amazed, and I listened to it again. Russell helped me understand the true nature of meditation. I knew it was simple enough to try. I felt it was powerful enough to make a difference in my life.

This notion of prayer and meditation is as old as *The Bible*; yet, for some reason, meditation is still seen as an evil practice. It isn't! Oprah Winfrey and others owe a debt of gratitude to New Thought thinkers like Rev. Dr. Johnnie Colemon, Bishop Barbara Lewis King, and Michael Bernard Beckwith, who've taught thousands in Chicago, Atlanta, Los Angeles, and beyond that prayer is speaking to God and meditation is listening to God. There are over seventy biblical references to the practice of meditation, including these verses:

> "And Isaac went out to meditate in the field at the eventide: and he lifted up his eyes, and saw, and, behold, the camels were coming." Genesis 24:63

> "Be still, and know that I am God…" Psalm 46:10

> "Blessed is the man that walketh not in the counsel of the ungodly, nor standeth in the way of sinners, nor sitteth in the seat of the scornful. But his delight is in the law of the LORD; and in his law doth he meditate day and night. And he shall be like a tree planted by the rivers of water, that bringeth forth his fruit in his season; his leaf also shall not wither; and whatsoever he doeth shall prosper." Psalm 1:1-3

"This book of the law shall not depart out of thy mouth; but thou shalt meditate therein day and night, that thou mayest observe to do according to all that is written therein: for then thou shalt make thy way prosperous, and then thou shalt have good success." Joshua 1:8.

I took time to delve deeper into meditation and determine what it meant for me. I turned to the words of Jesus:

"And when thou prayest, thou shalt not be as the hypocrites are: for they love to pray standing in the synagogues and in the corners of the streets, that they may be seen of men. Verily I say unto you, They have their reward. But thou, when thou prayest, enter into thy closet, and when thou hast shut thy door, pray to thy Father which is in secret; and thy Father which seeth in secret shall reward thee openly. But when ye pray, use not vain repetitions, as the heathen do: for they think that they shall be heard for their much speaking. Be not ye therefore like unto them: for your Father knoweth what things ye have need of, before ye ask him." Matthew 6:5-8

I read different versions of scriptures related to prayer and meditation. The more I read, the more I saw the connection between prayer and meditation. Matthew's story of Jesus telling us how to pray sounded a lot like meditation to me. Jesus was saying to us, "Go to a quiet place, sit still, shut out the world, and go within." After all, "The kingdom of God is within you." Luke 17:21.

I'd been meditating for years and didn't know it! I'd sit still and focus on my breathing. Sometimes I'd pray in tongues (also called glossolalia) for half an hour and then sit in silence afterwards listening for a word from God. I didn't have any idols. There weren't any demons. It was just me and God.

This listening for a word from God didn't happen overnight. I had to develop patience as I listened for the "still, small voice" the way I was taught to do when I grew up in church. Unfortunately, many of us have been taught we'd only get to hear that voice in church. I didn't know and wasn't taught I could hear from God when I meditated. Thankfully, I've learned patience, "But they that wait upon the LORD shall renew their strength; they shall mount up with wings as eagles; they shall run, and not be weary; and they shall walk, and not faint." Isaiah 40:31.

Waiting on the Lord involved service, expectation, and patience. I quickly learned there is strength in patience. When life comes at us fast and we're beaten down, we must take time to gather ourselves. This may mean finding new strategies for coping. My old ways of coping had left me out of sorts with failed relationships and poor health. I was making poor choices again and desired a different outcome.

*What must I do? What steps should I take?*
I chose to meditate.

Trusting God, that's what meditation is about. I remember the first time I used the GPS on my smartphone. I was headed along a familiar road when my GPS offered me a different route instead of the way I'd normally travel. I knew those roads like the lines on my palms; I could travel them without thinking.

*Not today! I've lived here all my life!*

My GPS was hard at work on things I simply couldn't—or didn't—know. My GPS updated itself constantly with real-time traffic information. My GPS had gotten word of a car crash causing major delays on the road up ahead. It offered me another route.

*Where is this thing trying to send me? I've used this shortcut for years!*

It offered. I declined. I was in charge. I knew best. That is all.

I didn't take my GPS's suggested detour based on my experiences. I was confident I knew the best way. I was sure I was plugged into the latest happenings. After all, this was familiar territory. My stubborn determination added almost an hour to my trip. I learned to trust the GPS because it was advising me of the best route to take using real-time data.

Praying and meditating regularly are like using a GPS. Through prayer and meditation, we deepen our patience and connect with God, the Good, as

# THE JOURNEY TO AUTHENTICITY

The Source. Prayer, mediation, and any practice of looking within give us up-to-date information. We can then determine what to do, decide where to go, and address the challenges ahead.

Prayer and meditation have proven to be powerful tools for me to address challenges and obstacles. They slow things down a bit, and then I think about things differently. We cannot approach the same task, situation, or challenge the same way we have in the past. Each experience is unique and presents new opportunities for growth and development. We won't realize these new opportunities for change if we're moving based on familiarity and past judgments. Our memory recall cannot account for the traffic delays, detours, and road closings in our lives.

We benefit from our own GPS: Prayer and Meditation. What we recall—without our internal GPS—may lead us into more crashes, congestion, and delays. When we pray and meditate, we listen to God's presence within us. Listening to your inner voice provides a clear passage on the road of life. It may not be easy, but it won't be impossible to travel.

The art of meditation goes hand in hand with patience because meditation teaches patience. It's in waiting that we get the lesson and a blessing. It is in waiting that we renew our strength. The art of meditation renewed my purpose and my passion. My vision came alive once more. Through meditation, I gained insights into who and whose I am. I realized I hadn't watered-down or changed my gifts, calling, and mission. I reclaimed faith and patience as essential to seeing my desires come to pass.

Adding meditation to my prayer practice changed my life. And as important as meditation is to who I have become today, I keep my meditation practice fresh by *choosing* to do it every day. Let me explain: Sometimes when we *have* to do something, it becomes a burden, a chore, or an obligation. By *choosing* to meditate when I wake up in the morning, I make a conscious decision to maintain a spiritual connection with the Universe and with God. By *choosing* to meditate, I *LiveLifeLiv*.

---

## LifeWork: Be Patient

We see *Quick Oil Change* shops everywhere because routine oil changes are inexpensive forms of preventative maintenance. We change the oil because doing so ensures the engines get lubricated and allows them to last longer and run smoother. Regular oil changes keep our vehicles in good working order and road-ready. The practice of prayer and meditation—developed with patience—is like fresh oil. Without consistent prayer and meditation, we become rigid, erratic, and unreliable. We experience breakdowns in the worst ways and at the wrong times. Life is filled with challenges and change. They are constants.

I encourage you to take some time with these three *LifeWork* assignments. With all *LifeWork*, you get out of them what you put into them.

1.  We know that tension, anxiety, impatience, and other forms of emotional distress can block good things from us. What might you gain from being patient? What's been your understanding of meditation? How could meditation practice benefit you? What will you do now to be patient?

2.  We live in a world where quick reactions to enduring questions are praised over deliberate, thoughtful responses and solutions. Slowing down really allows us to do more. If being patient is a challenge for you, what practical steps will you take now to develop your capacity for patience? For example, the next time you're in a store, get in the longest line and wait. What do you notice about your reaction to waiting in the long line? What can you do to deepen your practice of patience?

3.  Every time you feel yourself growing impatient with others, ask yourself, "why?" Look at your own thinking. Why are you in such a hurry? Take a moment to breathe; it

slows down your thinking and allows you to see the other person with compassion. Think about the times when people have been impatient with you. How did it make you feel? How might you use those experiences to change how you treat others?

**Lifework Affirmation**
*I am patient!*

# 9 BE OPEN

*Let go of certainty. The opposite isn't uncertainty. It's openness, curiosity and a willingness to embrace paradox, rather than choose up sides. The ultimate challenge is to accept ourselves exactly as we are, but never stop trying to learn and grow.*
— Tony Schwartz

It seems—more and more—people view the world in polar opposites. Rights and wrongs. Lies and Truths. Good and Bad. Good presidential candidates; bad presidential candidates. Not only do we have opposing positions, we also have fixed positions. A number of people see life as fixed and unchanging. The truth is this: *Anything that isn't growing isn't living.* We don't need to go far afield to see this in action. When our families don't birth babies, we see families die out. When our churches don't welcome new members into the fold, we see faith communities wipe out. Anything that isn't growing isn't living. And if it isn't living, it's dead.

We keep things fresh, alive, and open when we notice, analyze, request, and reveal. I remember studying Romans, Chapter 1, one night in Bible study. It was a Wednesday night at Third Baptist Church and the pastor, Rev. Delmar Rutherford Walters, Sr. was holding court minutes before Bible study. We assembled in the fellowship hall on folding chairs. I think the chairs' designers were a part of a global conspiracy to torture our behinds as we sat motionless. *Why didn't the chairs have more padding?* Surely, the cushion-to-Bible study time ratio needed adjusting.

I'd just arrived in a 1987 *Plymouth Horizon*, a gift for me and my brother. It had been a few weeks since we received our gift and we were still recovering from the surprise. My Dad told us he'd bought us the car because we were always running back and forth to church. We lived a country mile away and always seemed to need a ride home. It was time we took on the responsibility of driving ourselves...and paying the car note! I felt independent and carefree.

Rev. Walters turned the well-thumbed pages of his study Bible to the first chapter of *Romans*. We learned this book was the Apostle Paul's letter to the Christians who lived in Rome. Paul had written the letter to teach the Romans how to live for God. He wrote it to give them a concrete theological foundation on which to construct their faith. Paul wanted them to know their good deeds would not grant them salvation. Salvation, according to Paul, was available to the Romans through their faith in God's righteousness.

Rev. Walters talked about our sinful nature and the outcomes of sinful living.

*"In Romans 6:23, Paul tells us 'For the wages of sin is death; but the gift of God is eternal life through Jesus Christ our Lord.'"*

One well-placed, *"Amen, pastor!"* was all he'd need to settle into what would become a sermonette.

"And *The Bible* says we must seek right relationship with our God. Amen?"

"Amen, pastor!"

"...that's the only way you'll be saved! You've got to confess Jesus as the Lord of your life. Then you've gotta believe Jesus died on the cross and was put in a borrowed tomb. Then you've gotta believe God raised Jesus from the dead. If you have faith and believe these things, you will be saved!"

"Preach, preacher."

*This makes sense.*

I was a Bible study regular. I was there when others didn't show up. I loved learning and my pastor was giving us a good Word that night. It got good to Rev. Walters and he shifted his pace. His voice crept up an octave.

"We cannot be conformed to this world."

I couldn't help but wonder who would actually get into Heaven. Rev. Walters, unfazed, continued rattling off Paul's lists of things we mustn't do as Christians. I heard the words "effeminate" and "homosexual" followed by "abomination." I was 16 years old. I understood the connection between effeminate and feminine. Although I'd experimented with boys and girls over the years, I knew I was OK.

*I ain't feminine. I play sports. I gotta girlfriend. He ain't talking about me.*

Although I didn't have an exact definition of abomination, I knew it wasn't a word used to describe anything positive.

"Let's tell the truth and shame the devil: An abomination, my God, is worse than sin. Amen?"

"Amen! You betta say that!"

"...and homosexuality is something our God hates!"

Rev. Walters elaborated more and more while my head spun with a whirlwind of questions: *Wait, God hates me? How can He? I didn't choose this. Am I going to Hell? What can I do? Why can't He save me?*

I didn't want to go to Hell. Years before, Rev. Bradley Tucker Bowers III from Mary Magdalene Baptist Church had vividly sketched the treacherous landscape of Hell. Eternal flames. Scorpions snipping at your ears. Worms transforming your body into a maze of exits and entrances. Screams and weeping. Burning brimstone. All of these raw images flooded my imagination as I sat there on uncomfortable folding chairs while Rev. Walters brought the Bible study to a close.

I'd enjoyed intimate moments with boys for a while. The shock of learning I'd been sinning each week for almost six years was overwhelming. It seemed as if I'd purchased multiple one-way tickets on the express train to Hell. I felt detached from my body. I robotically spoke to just enough people to be polite before rushing to the safety of my car. Once inside, I cried and I cried. I sobbed the entire seven-mile trip home.

*God doesn't love me. I'm gonna die and split Hell wide open when I get there. I didn't know this was wrong.*

Just ahead I saw a familiar turn. I entered a heavily wooded area with majestic trees bending their fingertips to canopy the road.

*I can end it now. No one will have to worry about my sins. If I hit the tree at the perfect angle, it'll be a quick death.*

And there I was cruising along a three-mile stretch of road, debating the level of sin I'd commit as a gay man versus the sin of killing myself. I still had questions about the sin of homosexuality, but I knew suicide was a clear abomination. I figured I'd be better off taking my chances on getting delivered from homosexuality.

My mom was sewing in the den when I arrived. I told her I really needed to talk with Rev. Walters. I found a quiet place and dialed. Rev. Walters's wife, The First Lady, answered.

"No, son, Pastor, hasn't returned from tonight's Bible study."

"Yes, ma'am. I really would like to talk to him...it's about tonight's Bible study." I couldn't contain my tears any more.

"Mitchell, I'll have him call as soon as he gets in. You be blessed now, you hear?"

It wasn't long before the phone rang. Rev. Walters's voice had dropped to its normal octave. I told him about my questions. We talked about my thoughts on my drive home. For almost an hour he encouraged me and prayed for me. I was on the ledge that night and my pastor kept me from making a choice I knew I'd regret.

If life were uncomplicated, I would've been able to say I changed the moment my pastor prayed for my soul. If life unfolded just as I'd have it, I would've been able to say all my urges and fantasies about men disappeared that night. Life in some distant land or in a time long gone would've had folks laying hands and speaking in tongues, I'd fast and tarry, and then, "Shazam!" I'd become a hot-blooded, woman-loving man. That just wasn't the case. Life had more surprises in store for me.

Even with my biblical knowledge about homosexuality, I was compelled to go beyond the sex and intimacy to something greater: freedom. My struggle with my identity was far from being over. There were parts of me I couldn't deny without losing my mind. I had to lose myself to find myself.

I saw a chasm grow between me and God. I'd let two ministers—Rev. Walters and Rev. Bowers —close me off from God, the Good and All-

Loving. Between the vivid description of Hell on one hand and the demonization of same gender love on the other, I entered a cycle of trauma that took years to break. Thankfully, even in moments of intense doubt, I remained open to God's Love and Truth. Years later, I wish I'd know to flip just a few more chapters ahead to find my healing. If I had thought about it that fateful night at Third Baptist Church, I would've turned to Romans, Chapter 8:

"Who shall separate us from the love of Christ? shall tribulation, or distress, or persecution, or famine, or nakedness, or peril, or sword?

As it is written, For thy sake we are killed all the day long; we are accounted as sheep for the slaughter.

Nay, in all these things we are more than conquerors through him that loved us.

For I am persuaded, that neither death, nor life, nor angels, nor principalities, nor powers, nor things present, nor things to come,

Nor height, nor depth, nor any other creature, shall be able to separate us from the love of God, which is in Christ Jesus our Lord." Romans 8:35-39.

Who shall separate me from the love of God? Nothing shall separate me from the love of God. Not two trusted preachers. Not well-meaning well-wishers. Nothing! It didn't take me too long to be persuaded that neither wife, nor holier-than-thou saints, nor things present, nor things to come, nor height, nor depth, nor any decision I made shall be able to separate me from the love of God.

As much as I knew and learned about God, there was always much more I'd hope to learn about Him. Many Christians live their lives as same-gender loving people who are separated from the love of God. To make strides towards authenticity and freedom, I had to reconcile my faith. I had to reconsider my relationship with God, the Universe, and Scripture. I had to do my own work.

Around 2009, I drastically changed my beliefs and I shared what I'd learned with my congregation. The change was so sudden; many people just couldn't cope with an earthquake of devastation to their religious foundations. I remember one member cradling his head, whispering, "I just don't get this, pastor." I had to honor them where they were. Their views, beliefs, and opinions were valid. I'd been researching and studying for a while. I'd been open; I had to remember to be patient. I quickly learned how judgmental I'd been in the past.

One big change I made was understanding that God is bigger than Christianity. There are many paths to God as Infinite Spirit. Before my awakening, I believed people who didn't accept Jesus Christ as Savior and Lord—or couldn't because they just didn't know Him—were doomed to Hell for eternity. The saints hit the door when I revealed my thinking about Hell. They weren't buying the "Hell doesn't exist" slogan I was shouting. I hadn't begun to share my thinking about homosexuality and *The Bible*. That would do them in! Somehow, I thought my members would excitedly receive this Good News. They weren't moved; just over 60% of the congregation left my church in the four months between August and November 2009.

I realized Apostle Paul's letter was rooted in fear. We found comfort and unity in our fears. We were afraid of Hell. We didn't want to disappoint our family and church. We were bullied into checking our brains at the doors of the sanctuary. We were encouraged to fit in by doing as we were told. We were afraid to ask too many questions. And the few questions we did ask went unanswered because someone saw them as expressions of doubt. I now agreed with Astrophysicist Neil deGrasse Tyson, who said, "No one is dumb who is curious. The people who don't ask questions remain clueless throughout their lives." I had to release myself from the teachings of my past. I found the answers in *The Bible* and within. I'd heard enough of the *fire-and-brimstone* Christianity; my heart was ready for scriptures that make us free.

One's interpretation of *The Bible* remains among the greatest challenges to understanding it. Regardless of the scriptures people read or recite, the verses are always left to interpretation. Some people are literalists and interpret *The Bible* to mean exactly what it says at *face value*. Many modern-day Christians still maintain a literal interpretation of *The Bible*. They refuse any explanation of metaphorical or metaphysical interpretations. Their *Bible* is always right and they don't want to be confused with the truth.

Many modern-day Christians would pass out and go on to Glory if they knew there are well over 100 versions of *The Bible* (including their beloved King James Version). Some Bibles include certain books others exclude. Some Bibles use words that radically change the meaning and message of scripture. For example, Matthew 6:13, of the King James Version, was translated by scholars to read, *"And lead us not into temptation*, but deliver us from evil: For thine is the kingdom, and the power, and the glory, forever. Amen." Notice how it changes with this contemporary translation, *"And leave us not in temptation*, but deliver us from evil: For thine is the kingdom, and the power, and the glory, forever. Amen."

We must remember that *The Bible* is Near Eastern in origin. It's filled with powerful accounts of spiritual teachings and miraculous events. We must look at *The Bible* with different eyes if we seek to understand the parables and allusions found inside. In *Let There Be Light: The Seven Keys,* Dr. Rocco Errico outlines the seven keys to understanding *The Bible*. Dr. Errico's framework explains how the Aramaic Language, Idioms,

Mysticism, Culture, Psychology, Symbolism, and Amplification clarify much of what the divinely inspired writers were attempting to communicate.

I've learned I must be open and welcoming to all. I must be inviting and receptive. I realize we are the hands and feet of God. When people interact with us and witness our faith walk, we become the face of God. *Who are we being when we interact with others?* I strive to be nomadic in my thinking. I remain open to the possibilities. I question everything. I answer the question; then, I question the answer. Over the years, I've been open to new things and new ways of seeing the world as a gift from God. Because I am open to God's goodness, I have attracted new people, new experiences, and new opportunities.

---

## LifeWork: Be Open

I am not the Mitchell L. Jones I was ten years ago, five years ago, or even five days ago. I am free from the bondage of limited views and polar opposites. *Anything that isn't growing isn't living.* And if it isn't living, it's dead. My aim is to *LiveLifeLiv.* Today, I am open to experiencing a diversity of ideas and beliefs. I've been open to discovering the presence of the Lord wherever people are gathered. I've been to Unity and Universalist Unitarian churches. I've experienced New Thought Truth Centers and Catholic masses. I've spoken at PFLAG (Parents and Friends of Lesbians and Gays) meetings. I've attended same gender loving events without hesitation. I couldn't have arrived at this point had I remained the judgmental hypocrite I was for so many years.

To be open is to allow yourself to evolve. It's something that takes patience and love. The people around you may not understand your growth. They may leave you hurt and alone. But opening oneself to the unknown is also exciting. I'm ready to continue the healing adventure. Are you?

I encourage you to take some time with these three *LifeWork* assignments. With all *LifeWork*, you get out of them what you put into them.

1. We must be willing to grow and learn. When we do so, we become open and discover new paths. What will you commit to doing now to open your mind to the possibilities in your life? These actions don't need to be bold. They can be as simple as taking a different way home from work, trying a new restaurant, or visiting a local museum. Who knows what you may discover!

2. Sometimes we rush to judge a new friend or love interest. How are you limiting your relationships by being closed? What can you do now to be open to understanding their points of view, without rushing to

conclusions? How might this shift in thinking change your life experiences?

3. Take a moment to revisit your childhood upbringing and your spiritual foundations. What things were you taught back then that now imprison you? Who taught you those beliefs? What would life be like if you release those beliefs and forgave those who taught them to you? What will you do now to embark upon a new journey where you experience healing from a life of hurt?

**Lifework Affirmation**
***I am open!***

JONES

# 10 BE LOVING

*Thou shalt love thy neighbor as thyself.*
— Matthew 22:39

In 2004, I wasn't loving myself and this manifested itself in many ways. My sermons exhibited the internal struggle I was living each day. I still saw my sexuality as a flaw and not a gift. It was something I needed to pray out. I saw it as a stain on my bloodline. I feared I'd pass it on to my children, nieces, and nephews, just as I believed at that time that it had passed on to me. Someone needed to gain victory over the "curse" and stop it from passing generation to generation. It had to be me.

During that time I peppered my sermons with self-hatred and loathing. Sometimes these feelings were vague and veiled; other times they were direct and cutting. An example of my old way of thinking is in this sermon from that time:

*I was a practicing homosexual at one time. If you know me and you didn't know, you know now. I'm delivered now, and I want you to get yours too. When I grew up in church they didn't talk about homosexuality. I did not know that it was wrong, until our church got a new pastor that talked about that kind of controversial sin. I thought, "Wow, the truth is homosexuality is wrong." In spite of what I had been exposed to my first response was, "Lord, you know who and what I am."...Needless to say, it became a natural inclination to me—natural instinct.*

*I learned early on that when we don't know what's wrong (sin) we follow what we feel (flesh). However, after I heard the truth (the Word), I got convicted (by the Holy Spirit) and that's when the struggle began. There is no struggle when you do not know the truth because you do not have any conviction or feel guilty about anything. The struggle began when I heard the truth. It didn't get better for me. It got worse!*

*I came to a time when I could see a beautiful woman, and she didn't even move me. I said, "Hold on God…I'm about to cross a line here." The Holy Spirit in me said, "If you cross this line, you are not coming back." Nonetheless, I kept going to the clubs. I kept hanging out knowing that I didn't have any business being there.*

*I'm talking about fighting! Some of you go places, and you are not fighting. Some of you are having trouble at home, your marriage is a wreck, and you are not trying to fight. You get on the phone telling everybody, and none of them can help you. You have not said a thing to your husband. You have not said anything to your wife. You have problems with your children. You are not talking to your children. You are talking to everyone else and none of them can do anything for you. They have problems of their own to figure out.*

*I discovered by sincerely seeking the Lord through prayer, fasting, and consecration that I was a homosexual because someone in my bloodline was doing the same thing and didn't deal with it. They didn't expose it! Therefore, they didn't get delivered, and I couldn't be delivered. Praise God that I can say to you today that I am delivered. I purposed in my heart that I would get delivered so that my nephews, my sons, my grandsons, and my great-grandsons wouldn't have to put up with this Hell. Yes, indeed!*

*I asked God to show me what happened to bring all of this upon me if I wasn't born that way. Why did I ask? He took me to the day. He took me to the room. He took me to the moment. He took me right to the summer afternoon that I decided to view a pornographic magazine with my cousin. I thought it was innocent at the time. The Holy Spirit of God said to me, "That's where you opened the door." I accepted it by saying, "OK, God. I opened the door."*

*So, God took me to the door that I opened. I repented that instant. Then He showed me something else. It had to do with what I was trying to get through. He reminded me how my aunt, who was extremely forgetful, could not even remember her childhood. He further explained to me that it was because of some traumatic events that happened in her life that she was blocking out of her mind. These are events of which she has never spoken. Today she is a senior citizen still bound because she won't expose the sin or the curse that manifested itself through the bloodline in her generation.*

*The thought pattern for her is one that says, "I can't mess up the family name and our family reputation." You know how we are. Our family has a reputation to uphold as a part of the elite group, and what are people going to think about our family if we expose the "secret." All of our families are imperfect in some way or another and have some dysfunction in them.*

*I prayed, "Lord, take this thing from me. Take the whole appetite. I don't want it." You should know that He didn't do what I asked Him to do immediately. I thought I was less than a Christian. I thought I was not walking in the power of God. I thought God was mad at me. I thought that He was aiming at me. I thought He wasn't going to use me. I thought He wasn't going to bless me. Then He said to me (get this), "If I take this from you, you will not know My power."*

# THE JOURNEY TO AUTHENTICITY

*When I first began to walk in deliverance, I thought I was better than those who were still struggling. I would look at them with the attitude that said, "I am not struggling with that anymore...I don't know you...Who are you?" We tend to lift ourselves up in self-righteousness. "Pride goeth before destruction, and an haughty spirit before a fall." Proverbs 16:18.*

*When we overcome something that still holds other people captive, we should consider that we are one step from being in the same situation. Having said that, God allowed me to fall! I asked God, "Why did you do that? I thought you had taken homosexuality from me." He said, "When you got beside yourself (self-righteousness) I had to let you know that it was still there." Hold on, I was walking in deliverance, yet the thing was still there? I could not believe it.*

*Never forget where you have been in life. You see, I remember what I was, and I put all of my being into it at the time that I was a homosexual. Now that I am on the Lord's side and fully delivered, I have determined daily that I am going to put all of my being into who God has made me. You who were whoremongers that just loved men still have that same appetite. Don't fool yourself. You should not hug a man too long. Your flesh is still your flesh and it remembers the touch. So how do you rule your flesh? You have to pray and study as many times as you wash your body.*

*We no longer have an excuse because we have the knowledge of the truth. When we see the knowledge of the truth, walk therein. You now know how to stay delivered. You now know how to get delivered. I am challenging you, particularly those of you who are struggling with your sexuality, to get your house in order. Save your children from so much headache and stress...From here on you have to determine that you are going to get it right. You are not going to go on in the fullness of your destiny and purpose if you are not going to get it right. That's reality. I rejoice with you because your best days are ahead!*

Talk about a walking contradiction! And this was a mild sermon. The most detrimental thing passed on wasn't my same-gender attraction. What *was* passed on was fear and twisted thinking. I fed on this deadly diet of self-hate year after year. Before I learned about the *sin of homosexuality*, I was a child who lived without fear of Hell. I was genuine, a good person, and I loved myself. Then I bought into all of the scriptures that separated me from the love of God.

The lives of my children are what're most important to me now. I must instill in them the act of being loving and open, without judgement. I must instill the knowledge that they can always change the path they are on. I have told them it's OK to cry. It's OK to make what others will call *mistakes*; but they mustn't let those choices hinder them or block them from their divine purpose. I've shown them that forgiveness and courage are necessary if we desire to be loving.

The *Eight Secrets* aren't material things. Courage, vulnerability, steadfastness, forgiveness, gratitude, patience, openness, and love are all states of being. They are free to us because they come from within. When we use the *Eight Secrets*, we honor God's gifts within us. You can access the *Eight Secrets* whenever and wherever you choose to do so. Just like I did. Just like I am.

----

## LifeWork: Be Loving

*Be Loving* is the foundation of the *Eight Secrets to Getting the Life You Desire.* It is essential for living an authentic life. The power of love is a central part of the ministry of Jesus who said, "Thou shalt love the Lord thy God with all thy heart, and with all thy soul, and with all thy mind. This is the first and great commandment. And the second is like unto it, Thou shalt love thy neighbor as thyself. On these two commandments hang all the law and the prophets." Matthew 22:37-40.

Once you love yourself, knowing your purpose becomes clear. I am here to inspire, influence, and encourage people to motivate themselves through sharing my story with others, encouraging them to be themselves, and to do what they've come here to do with success and authenticity. Together, we *LiveLifeLiv*!

I encourage you to take some time with these three *LifeWork* assignments. With all *LifeWork*, you get out of them what you put into them.

1.  To be loving, we must first love ourselves and believe we are amazing. We must aspire to be ourselves and no one else. We must desire new and improved versions of ourselves every day. Once we love ourselves, we can authentically love others. Where have you been withholding love? Why have you done so? Who would benefit from your loving kindness? What will you do to be loving? When is the last time you wrote in your Gratitude Journal? Have you made any Gratitude Calls?

2.  Love is often best expressed as an action. Think about a talent of yours you haven't used in a while. How might that untapped talent express love to others? If you enjoy painting, volunteer your services to a shelter for children and brighten their days with your gift. If you have a gift of singing or playing instruments, dust off your guitar and call a local Senior Adult Daycare Center. Give them a concert of love. What will you do now to lovingly share your gifts with others?

3.  Take a moment to look at yourself in the mirror. Notice your eyes and nose. Notice

your ears and lips. Notice your skin. Notice each part of your body. Take moments to soak in how wonderfully you're made. Accept yourself as you are, right now. Now, give yourself a big hug and tell yourself how much you love you!

**Lifework Affirmation**
*I am loving!*

# JONES

# SPEAKING AND CONSULTING

**Pastor Mitchell L. Jones** effectively blends candor and wit to engage people in optimum personal growth. He leads retreats and facilitates workshops as a Life Coach and pastor. He is available for book signings and speaking engagements. For more information, or to be added to his mailing list, contact:

www. livelifeliv.com
209-809-1LIV

*more...*

**Dr. Tony Lamair Burks II** coaches and trains leaders for excellence. He is available for speaking engagements, workshops, and individual coaching. For more information contact:

info@LEADrightToday.com
www.LEADrightToday.com
619-796-6463

## ABOUT THE AUTHORS

**Pastor Mitchell L. Jones** grew up in Virginia in a large, God-fearing home with six brothers and two sisters, and loving parents who have been married nearly six decades. At the age of 5, Mitchell knew he was attracted to a boy and a girl in his kindergarten class. By the age of 11, he was intrigued by his sexuality and same-gender attraction; however, his sexual desires posed a problem given his strict Southern Baptist upbringing. Mitchell's same-gender attraction was in direct conflict with his religious upbringing, so he repressed his feelings thinking he was going through "a phase."

At 23, he began pastoring a non-denominational church in Richmond, Virginia, and often preached sermons condemning himself and others to an eternity in Hell. Mitchell met and married a young mother of three and the new family grew to include two more children. After 13 years of pastoring, counseling, and teaching, Mitchell plumbed the depths of his religious upbringing and studied the teachings of Jesus, discovering and expressing a multi-faceted spirituality that radically shifted his sermons. His once traditional religious teachings became progressive and inclusive, which, ironically, resulted in a mass exodus of members from his congregation.

Mitchell redefined his ministry based on his new understanding of Scripture. Today, he leads Bible-study groups, helping others understand living a purposeful life and embarking upon their spiritual path for optimum personal growth. With a renewed sense of clarity and personal acceptance, Mitchell ended his five-year marriage to live an authentic life. He's embraced his true self through years of discovery and actualization and now realizes the power of God's love in his life.

———

**Dr. Tony Lamair Burks II** is an award-winning education expert who helps individuals and organizations as a thought partner and coach. A Fulbrighter and fellow of the British-American Project, he was recognized by *NU·tribe Magazine* as one of *Six HBCU Grads You Should Know* and was honored with the *Phaedra Parks S.O.S. Save Our Sons Award for Empowerment and Service.* He is a graduate of Morehouse College, Trevecca Nazarene University, and the University of North Carolina at Greensboro, and he is a student at the Barbara King School of Ministry. He is the author of *Bought Wisdom: Tales of Living and Learning.*

www.ingramcontent.com/pod-product-compliance
Lightning Source LLC
Chambersburg PA
CBHW071135280326
41935CB00010B/1233